Pro Perl Programming

From Professional to Advanced

William "Bo" Rothwell

Apress®

Pro Perl Programming: From Professional to Advanced

William "Bo" Rothwell
San Diego, CA, USA

ISBN-13 (pbk): 978-1-4842-5604-6   ISBN-13 (electronic): 978-1-4842-5605-3
https://doi.org/10.1007/978-1-4842-5605-3

Managing Director, Apress Media LLC: Welmoed Spahr
Acquisitions Editor: Steve Anglin
Development Editor: Matthew Moodie
Coordinating Editor: Mark Powers

Cover designed by eStudioCalamar

Cover image designed by Freepik (www.freepik.com)

Distributed to the book trade worldwide by Springer Science+Business Media New York, 233 Spring Street, 6th Floor, New York, NY 10013. Phone 1-800-SPRINGER, fax (201) 348-4505, e-mail orders-ny@springer-sbm.com, or visit www.springeronline.com. Apress Media, LLC is a California LLC and the sole member (owner) is Springer Science + Business Media Finance Inc (SSBM Finance Inc). SSBM Finance Inc is a **Delaware** corporation.

For information on translations, please e-mail editorial@apress.com; for reprint, paperback, or audio rights, please email bookpermissions@springernature.com.

Apress titles may be purchased in bulk for academic, corporate, or promotional use. eBook versions and licenses are also available for most titles. For more information, reference our Print and eBook Bulk Sales web page at http://www.apress.com/bulk-sales.

Any source code or other supplementary material referenced by the author in this book is available to readers on GitHub via the book's product page, located at www.apress.com/9781484256046. For more detailed information, please visit http://www.apress.com/source-code.

Printed on acid-free paper

To all Perl Mongers, new and old.

Table of Contents

About the Author

At the impressionable age of 14, **William "Bo" Rothwell** crossed paths with a TRS-80 Micro Computer System (affectionately known as a "Trash 80"). Soon after, the adults responsible for Bo made the mistake of leaving him alone with the TRS-80. He immediately dismantled it and held his first computer class, showing his friends what made this "computer thing" work. Since this experience, Bo's passion for understanding how computers work and sharing this knowledge with others has resulted in a rewarding career in IT training. His experience includes Linux, Unix, DevOps tools, orchestration, security, and programming languages such as Perl, Python, Tcl, and Bash.

Bo can be contacted via LinkedIn: `www.linkedin.com/in/bo-rothwell`.

About the Technical Reviewer

Germán González-Morris is a polyglot software architect/engineer and has been 20+ years in the field, with knowledge in Java(EE), Spring, Haskell, C, Python, and JavaScript, among others. He works with web distributed applications. Germán loves math puzzles (including reading Knuth) and swimming. He has tech-reviewed several books, including an application container book (WebLogic), as well as titles covering various programming languages (Haskell, TypeScript, WebAssembly, Math for coders, and regexp). You can find more details at his blog site (https://devwebcl.blogspot.com/) or Twitter account (@devwebcl).

CHAPTER 1

Intermediate Regular Expressions

Many people consider Perl to stand for **P**ractical **E**xtraction and **R**eport **L**anguage. This isn't strictly true as Larry Wall originally wanted to call the language Pearl, but he discovered there was already a language that went by that name (PEARL, or Process and experiment automation realtime language, a language created about ten years before Perl).

Practical Extraction and Report Language is actually a backronym, but it does serve to hammer home the point that Perl is well known as an extraction language. In order to extract data, you need good tools to filter data. That is where Regular Expressions step into the picture.

Perhaps more than any other language, Regular Expressions are a major part of Perl. This chapter focuses on "`intermediate-level`" Regular Expressions. Chapter 2 will continue the discussion while covering more advanced Regular Expressions.

Review: Basic Regular Expressions

Basic Regular Expressions are discussed in the *Beginning Perl Programming: From Novice to Professional* book. The goal of this section is to provide a quick review of what is covered in that book.

If you are already familiar with these Regular Expressions, then skip to the next section. If not, then you should try the examples demonstrated in this section.

© William "Bo" Rothwell of One Course Source, Inc. 2020
W. "Bo" Rothwell, *Pro Perl Programming*, https://doi.org/10.1007/978-1-4842-5605-3_1

1

Basic operations

The following are the basic operations that can be performed with Regular Expressions:

op	Meaning
m	Pattern matching
s	Substituting
tr	Translating

Examples of basic operations:

```
DB<1> $line = "Today is a good day to learn Perl"
DB<2> if ($line =~ m/good/) {print "yes"}
yes
DB<3> $line =~ s/good/great/
DB<4> print $line
Today is a great day to learn Perl
DB<5> $line =~ tr/a-z/A-Z/
DB<6> print $line
TODAY IS A GREAT DAY TO LEARN PERL
```

Notes about the basic operators:

- Since matching is the most common operation, the "m" can be dropped in most cases:

  ```
  DB<1> if ($line =~ /good/) {print "yes"}
  ```

- If you perform matching, substitution, or translation on the default variable ($_), you can drop the "$var =~" portion of the command:

  ```
  DB<1> $_ = "Today is a good day to learn Perl"
  DB<2> if (/good/) {print "yes"}
  yes
  DB<3> s/good/great/
  DB<4> print $_
  ```

```
Today is a great day to learn Perl
DB<5> tr/a-z/A-Z/
DB<6> print $_
TODAY IS A GREAT DAY TO LEARN PERL
```

- The "y" operator is the same as the "tr" operator:

```
DB<1> print $line
Today is a great day to learn Perl
DB<2> $line =~ y/a-z/A-Z/
DB<3> print $line
TODAY IS A GREAT DAY TO LEARN PERL
```

Basic modifiers

The following basic modifiers were covered in the *Beginning Perl Programming: From Novice to Professional* book:

Modifier	Meaning
g	Global match or substitution
i	Case-insensitive match

The following code demonstrates the "g" modifier by showing how the behavior changes when the "g" modifier is used. Note that in the second substitution, all of the occurrences of dog are replaced with cat, while in the first substitution, only the first occurrence is replaced.

```
DB<1> $_="The dog ate the dog food"
DB<2> s/dog/cat/
DB<3> print
The cat ate the dog food
DB<4> $_="The dog ate the dog food"
DB<5> s/dog/cat/g
DB<6> print
The cat ate the cat food
```

The following code demonstrates "i" modifier by showing how the behavior changes when the "i" modifier is used. Note how in the first match attempt that "perl" without the "i" modifier does not match "Perl".

```
DB<1> $_="This is a good day to learn Perl"
DB<2> if (/perl/) {print "yes"}
DB<3> if (/perl/i) {print "yes"}
yes
```

Basic metacharacters

Perl supports a rich collection of metacharacters. Each metacharacter is used to represent other characters that you want to match within a string. The following chart summarizes the metacharacters that were covered in the *Beginning Perl Programming: From Novice to Professional* book:

Char	Meaning
*	Represents the previous character repeated zero or more times
+	Represents the previous character repeated one or more times
{x,y}	Represents the previous character repeated x to y times
.	Represents exactly one character (any one character)
[ ]	Represents any single character listed within the bracket.
?	Represents an optional character. The char. prior to the "?" is optional
^	Represents the beginning of the line when it is the first character in the RE
$	Represents the end of the line when it is the last character in the RE
( )	Used to group an expression
|	Represents an "or" operator
\	Used to "escape" the special meaning of the above characters

Examples: The * and + characters

The following example of the * metacharacter matches "A", then zero or more "1" characters, followed by "Z":

```
DB<1> $_="Code: A111Z"
```

```
DB<2> if (/A1*Z/) {print "yes";} else {print "no"}
```
yes

Be careful when using the * metacharacter. The following will match every possible line because every line has "zero or more "3" characters":

```
DB<1> $_="Code: A111Z"
```

```
DB<2> if (/3*/) {print "yes";} else {print "no"}
```
yes

The danger of using the * metacharacter was demonstrated in the previous example. In most cases, it is better to use the + character because it ensures at least one character is matched:

```
DB<1> $_="Code: A111Z"
```

```
DB<2> if (/3+/) {print "yes";} else {print "no"}
```
no
```
DB<1> $_="Code: A333Z"
```

```
DB<2> if (/3+/) {print "yes";} else {print "no"}
```
yes

Review the following table for some additional examples of the * and + metacharacters:

Example	Meaning
abc*	"ab" followed by zero or more c's
c*enter	Zero or more c's followed by "enter"
a*	Anything. Warning: This expression ALWAYS will find a match and will most likely match "nothing". Look for examples of this later in this unit

(*continued*)

Example	Meaning
abc+	"ab" followed by at least one (or more) c
c+enter	At least one c (or more) followed by "enter"
a+	Match one or more "a"

Examples: The { } characters

Suppose you don't want to just match zero or more of a character and you don't want to match one or more either. You want to match three, four, or five repeating characters. This is where the {} metacharacters are useful. The following example will match "A", then three, four, or five "1" characters, followed by "Z":

```
DB<1> $_="Code: A111Z"

DB<2> if (/A1{3,5}Z/) {print "yes";} else {print "no"}
yes
```

You can also leave the end value of the range "open". For example, the following will match "A", then three or more "1" characters, followed by "Z":

```
DB<1> $_="Code: A111Z"

DB<2> if (/A1{3,}Z/) {print "yes";} else {print "no"}
yes
```

If you place just a single integer in the {} metacharacters, you end up matching exactly that number of characters. For example, the following will match "A", then three "1" characters exactly, followed by "Z":

```
DB<1> $_="Code: A111Z"

DB<2> if (/A1{3}Z/) {print "yes";} else {print "no"}
yes
```

Review the following table for some additional examples of the { } metacharacters:

Example	Meaning
abc{3,5}	"ab" followed by three to five "c's"
abc{3,}	"ab" followed by three or more "c's"
abc{3}	"ab" followed by exactly three "c's"

Examples: The ? character

Another method that is sometimes used to repeat characters is the ? metacharacter. This metacharacter means "repeat the previous zero or one times". See the following for an example:

```
DB<1> $_="In the US it is color"

DB<2> if (/colou?r/) {print "yes";} else {print "no"}
yes
DB<3> $_="In other countries it is colour"

DB<4> if (/colou?r/) {print "yes";} else {print "no"}
yes
DB<3> $_="In no country is it colouuuur"

DB<4> if (/colou?r/) {print "yes";} else {print "no"}
no
```

Review the following table for some additional examples of the ? metacharacter:

Example	Meaning
abc?	Either "ab" or "abc"
colou?r	Either "color" or "colour"

Examples: The . character

If you want to match a single character, but you are not concerned what the character actually is, then you can use the . metacharacter. For example, the following will match "A", then exactly three characters, followed by "Z":

```
DB<1> $_="Code: A127Z"

DB<2> if (/A...Z/) {print "yes";} else {print "no"}
```
yes

Note that each . character must match exactly one character. The following examples demonstrate failed matches because the string contains only three characters between the "A" and "Z", which the Regular Expressions are trying to match two or four characters:

```
DB<1> $_="Code: A127Z"

DB<2> if (/A..Z/) {print "yes";} else {print "no"}
```
no
```
DB<2> if (/A....Z/) {print "yes";} else {print "no"}
```
no

Note that the . character does not match newline characters. This will be addressed later in this chapter.

Review the following table for some additional examples of the . metacharacter:

Example	Meaning
a.c	An "a" followed by any single character followed by a "c"
abc.	A "abc" followed by any single character
ab.*	A "ab" followed by zero or more of any character

Examples: The [ ] characters

Suppose you want to match a single character but not just any character. For example, suppose you want to match an "A", followed by three numbers, followed by a "Z". In this case you can use the [ ] characters to indicate you want to match a single character, but this single character must match one of a set of other characters:

```
DB<1> $_="Code: A127Z"
```

```
DB<2> if (/A[0123456789][0123456789][0123456789]Z/) {print "yes";} else
{print "no"}
```
yes

If the characters that are within the [ ] characters are in sequential order within the ASCII text table, a range can be used instead as shown in the next example:

```
DB<1> $_="Code: A127Z"
```

```
DB<2> if (/A[0-9][0-9][0-9]Z/) {print "yes";} else {print "no"}
```
yes

Don't forget that you can use { } characters to repeat patterns. The following example repeats the [0-9] three or more times:

```
DB<1> $_="Code: A127Z"
```

```
DB<2> if (/A[0-9]{3}Z/) {print "yes";} else {print "no"}
```
yes

You can also use the [ ] to match a character that is not part of a set of characters. For example, supposed you want to match any character that is not a lowercase alpha character, followed by three numbers, followed by a "Z" character:

```
DB<1> $_="Code: A127Z"
```

```
DB<2> if (/[^a-z][0-9][0-9][0-9]Z/) {print "yes";} else {print "no"}
```
yes

The ^ character means "not one of these characters" if it is the first character within the [ ] characters. Note that is must be the first character within the [ ] characters to have this special meaning.

Review the following table for some additional examples of the [ ] metacharacters:

Example	Meaning
[abc]xyz	Either an a, b, or c followed by "xyz"
[bca]xyz	Same as previous
[a-c]xyz	Same as previous

(continued)

Example	Meaning
[c-a]xyz	An improper range
[a-z]xyz	Any lowercase character followed by "xyz"
[A-Z]xyz	Any uppercase character followed by "xyz"
[A-z]xyz	Any lowercase or uppercase character **or** any of these characters: "[ ] ^ _ ' ' followed by "xyz"
[A-Za-z]xyz	Any uppercase or lowercase character followed by "xyz"
[A-Z][a-z]	A uppercase character followed by a lowercase character
gr[ae]y	Either "gray" or "grey"
[^A-Z]xyz	Any non-uppercase character followed by "xyz"
[abc^]xyz	First character is either "a", "b", "c", or "^" followed by "xyz"

Examples: The ^ and $ characters

Often you will want to search for a pattern at the beginning or end of the string. To match something at the beginning of a string, use the ^ character. For example, the pattern /^A127Z/ will attempt (and fail) to match "A127Z" at the beginning of the string, while pattern /^Code/ will attempt (and succeed) to match "Code" at the beginning of the string:

```
DB<1> $_="Code: A127Z"

DB<2> if (/^A127Z/) {print "yes";} else {print "no"}

DB<3> if (/^Code/) {print "yes";} else {print "no"}
yes
```

Conversely, the following examples will attempt to match A127Z and code at the end of the string:

```
DB<1> $_="Code: A127Z"

DB<2> if (/A127Z$/) {print "yes";} else {print "no"}
yes
DB<3> if (/Code$/) {print "yes";} else {print "no"}
```

Review the following table for some additional examples of the ^ and $ metacharacters:

Example	Meaning
^abc	"abc" found at the beginning of the line
abc$	"abc" found at the end of the line
^abc$	A line that just contains "abc"
^$	A blank line
^\^[^^]*$	A line that starts with a "^" and has no other "^" characters on it

Examples: The ( ) characters

The ( ) characters are used to group other characters together. For example, suppose you want to match a pattern like the following:

```
DB<1> $_="Code: A127127127Z"
```

You know there will be an "A", following by a collection of "127" patterns, followed by a "Z", but you don't know how many "127" patterns there will be. The following won't match because the + character is repeating just the previous character ("7", in this case):

```
DB<1> $_="Code: A127127127Z"

DB<2> if (/A127+Z/) {print "yes";} else {print "no"}
```

But, you can place ( ) characters around the "127" to have the + character apply to the group:

```
DB<1> $_="Code: A127127127Z"

DB<2> if (/A(127)+Z/) {print "yes";} else {print "no"}
yes
```

The ( ) characters are also used for a feature called backreferencing, which will be covered in a later section of this chapter.

Review the following table for some additional examples of the ( ) metacharacters:

Example	Meaning
(abc)*xyz	"abc" zero or more times followed by xyz
(abc)+xyz	"abc" one or more times followed by xyz
^(abc)+$	A line that contains one or more groups of "abc"

Examples: The | character

The | character acts as an "or" operator. It means "match the pattern that appears before the | character or the pattern that appears after the | character". For example:

```
DB<1> $_="Code: A127Z"

DB<2> if (/A127Z|B999Y/) {print "yes";} else {print "no"}
yes
 DB<3> $_="Code: B999Y"

 DB<4> if (/A127Z|B999Y/) {print "yes";} else {print "no"}
yes
```

In some cases, you want to limit the scope of the or operation. This can be done with ( ) characters:

```
DB<1> $_="Code: B999Y "

DB<2> if (Code: (/A127Z|B999Y/)) {print "yes";} else {print "no"}
yes
 DB<3> $_="Result: B999Y"

 DB<4> if (Code: (/A127Z|B999Y/)) {print "yes";} else {print "no"}
```

Examples: The \ character

The \ character is used to escape the meaning of special characters, such as *, + or ?. For example, suppose you want to match the following pattern: "Code: A*+[Z". The following won't work correctly:

```
DB<1> $_='Code: A*+[Z'
```

```
DB<2> if (/Code: A*+[Z/)  {print "yes";} else {print "no"}
Unmatched [ in regex; marked by <-- HERE in m/Code: A*+[ <-- HERE Z/ at
(eval 11)[/usr/share/perl5/perl5db.pl:732] line 2.
 at (eval 11)[/usr/share/perl5/perl5db.pl:732] line 2.
        eval 'no strict; ($@, $!, $^E, $,, $/, $\\, $^W) =
        @DB::saved;package main; $^D = $^D | $DB::db_stop;
if  (/Code: A*+[Z/)  {print "yes";} else {print "no"};
' called at /usr/share/perl5/perl5db.pl line 732
        DB::eval called at /usr/share/perl5/perl5db.pl line 3093
        DB::DB called at -e line 1
```

Instead, use \ before each RE character:

```
DB<1> $_='Code: A*+[Z'
```

```
DB<2> if (/Code: A\*\+\[Z/)  {print "yes";} else {print "no"}
yes
```

Regular Expressions classes

Regular Expression classes are used to create quick shortcuts to a set of characters. Commonly used RE classes are described in the following table:

Class	Matches
\w	Alphanumeric and underscore character
\d	Numeric
\s	Whitespace (space, tab, newline, formfeed, return)
\b	Word boundary (includes "whitespace", end/beginning of line, punctuation, etc.)
\W	Non-alphanumeric and underscore character
\D	Non-numeric characters
\S	Non-whitespace
\B	Non-word boundary

13

Examples: "\w" and "\d"

```
DB<1> $_="The code is A127Z"
DB<2> s/\d\d\d/---/
DB<3> print
The code is A---Z
DB<4> s/\w---\w/ZZZZZ/
DB<5> print
The code is ZZZZZ
```

Examples: "\s" and "\b"

```
DB<1> $_="This is fun"
DB<2> s/\sis\s/was/
DB<3> print
Thiswasfun
DB<4> $_="This is fun"
DB<5> s/\bis\b/was/
DB<6> print
This was fun
DB<7> $_="This is"
DB<8> if (/\sis\s/) {print "yes"}
DB<9> if (/\bis\b/) {print "yes"}
yes
```

Note that Perl also supports the following POSIX RE character classes:

Class	Matches
alpha	Any character of the alphabet
alnum	Any alphanumeric character
ascii	Any character in the ACSII text table
blank	A space or tab (horizontal)
cntrl	Any control character
digit	Any digit (same as [0-9])

(continued)

14

Class	Matches
lower	Any lowercase alphanumeric character
punct	Any punctuation character
space	Any whitespace character
upper	Any uppercase alphanumeric character
xdigit	Any hexadecimal digit
word	Same as \w

Note that these POSIX character classes are placed within "[::]". For example, [:alpha:]. Furthermore, these POSIX character classes are used with Perl [ ] characters, so to look for a lowercase character, followed by three numbers and then a lowercase character, you would use syntax like the following:

```
DB<1> $_='Code: a127z'
```

```
DB<2> if (/[[:lower:]][[:digit:]]{3}[[:lower:]]/) {print "yes";}
yes
```

Which will leave you wondering why not just use the following:

```
DB<1> $_='Code: a127z'
```

```
DB<2> if (/[a-z][\d{3}[a-z]/) {print "yes";}
yes
```

Often, using POSIX character class is a pain, but consider the following useful pattern that will match a single character that is either a digit or a punctuation character:

```
[[:digit:][:punct:]]
```

Backreferencing

Grouping can also be used to "backreference" patterns that have been matched. When Perl makes a match of characters within parentheses, what was matched can be referred back to

```
$var =~ s/^(...)abc/\1/;
```

The \1 means "match what was matched in the first group". A \2 means "match what was matched in the second group".

In addition to being able to backreference within the Regular Expression, Perl assigns what was matched within the grouping to special variables. The first group match is assigned to $1, the second group matched is assigned to $2, and so on.

```
$var =~ m/(abc..)/;
print $1;
```

The above will match the string "abc" followed by the next two characters and assign all five characters to the string $1.

Note   Future successful matches will cause these variables ($1, $2, etc.) to be overwritten.

Example #1: Backreferencing

The variables $1, $2, etc. can be used immediately after a successful pattern match. In this example, the user enters their first and last name. Then pattern matching is used to extract the first and last name and print them out in a different format (last name, first name):

```
#!perl
#1_back1.pl

print "Please enter your first and last name";
$_=<STDIN>;

if (m/(.*) (.*)/)  #ex: "Bob Smith"
{
    print "$2, $1\n";
}
```

Example #2: Backreferencing

In this example, the UNIX file /etc/group will be read into the script one line at a time and "parsed". Each line contains four fields of data that are separated by colons. This script will add the third field of each line and print the total:

```perl
#!perl
#1_back2.pl

open (GROUP, "</etc/group");

while (<GROUP>) {
    m/(.*):(.*):(.*):(.*)/;
    $total += $3;
}

print "Total: $total\n";
```

Note   The previous example isn't ideal because the values of $1, $2, and $4 are never used. A more efficient method for the **while** loop would be

---

```perl
while (<GROUP>) {
    m/.*:.*:(.*):/;
    $total += $1;
}
```

Example #3: Backreferencing

When you need to refer back to what was matched within the pattern itself, you need to use \1, \2, etc. instead of $1, $2, etc.:

```perl
#!perl
#1_back3.pl

print "Please enter a line: ";
$_=<STDIN>;
chomp $_;
```

```perl
if (/^(...).*\1$/) {print "$1\n";}

$junk="whatever";

if ($junk =~ /what/) {print "yes\n";}

print "$1\n";
```

Also note that when another pattern match is attempted and that match (or substitution) is *successful*, Perl will overwrite $1, $2, etc. even if you don't use parentheses.

Modifiers

In addition to the **g** and **i** modifiers discussed in *Beginning Perl Programming: From Novice to Professional,* there are other modifiers that change the behavior of a Regular Expression match. Modifiers for matching and substitution are different than the modifiers for translation. The following table provides a short description of commonly used matching and substation modifiers:

Mod	Meaning
e	Right-hand side of substitution is the code to evaluate
ee	Right-hand side of substitution is a string to evaluate and run as code. After completion, the return value is to be evaluated
g	Global match or substitution
gc	Doesn't reset the search position after a failed match
i	Case-insensitive match
m	Allows ^ and $ to match embed \n characters
o	Only compile the pattern once
p	Preserve the string matched such that ${^PREMATCH}, ${^MATCH}, and ${^POSTMATCH} are available for use after matching
s	Allows the ". " metacharacter to match newlines
x	Ignores whitespace in pattern and allows comments

Commonly used translation modifiers include the following:

Mod	Meaning
c	Complement the search list
d	Delete characters that are not replaced
s	Delete replaced characters that are duplicates

Note that not all of these modifiers are covered in detail in this chapter of the book.

The e modifier

When the **e** modifier is used, the right-hand (replacement) side of the substitution is evaluated as a Perl statement. The result of the statement is used as the replacement value:

```
DB<1> $var="123456789"
DB<2> $code="ABCDEFGHIJ"
DB<3> $code =~ s/J/chop $var/e
DB<4> print $code
ABCDEFGHI9
```

Note   The **e** modifier can only be used for substitution, not matching.

The d modifier

Normally when you have too many characters on the left side of a translation operation, you get "weird" results:

```
DB<1> $var = "This can become very odd"
DB<2> $var =~ tr/abcdefghij/ABC/
DB<3> print $var
TCCs CAn BCComC vCry oCC
```

In the preceding example, the **tr** operator replaced "a" with "A", "b" with "B", and all of the other characters ("c-j") with "C".

The **d** modifier means, "if something is matched and we don't specify what to replace it with, then remove it":

```
DB<1> $var="Lets cap this and remove all numbers: 1234567890"
DB<2> $var =~  tr/a-z0-9/A-Z/d
DB<3> print $var
LETS CAP THIS AND REMOVE ALL NUMBERS:
```

The s modifier

When the **s** modifier is used with the **tr** operator, it tells **tr** to delete duplicated characters that are replaced:

```
DB<1> $var="Exxtra chars are removed"
DB<2> $var =~ tr/xyz/XYZ/s
DB<3> print $var
EXtra chars are removed
```

Note   There is also an **s** modifier for matching and substitution that works differently than the **s** modifier for translation.

Other modifiers

Not all of the modifiers listed on the preceding page are discussed in detail in this course. The **g** and **i** modifiers were covered in the *Beginning Perl Programming: From Novice to Professional* book and are reviewed earlier in this chapter. Other modifiers will be introduced in future chapters.

**Try it!**

Execute the following command to enter the Perl Debugger environment:

```
perl -d -e "1;"
```

At the debugger prompt, execute the following Perl statements:

```
$code="Convert digits to ASCII: 1-2-3";
$code =~ s/1/ord(1)/e;
$code =~ s/2/ord(2)/e;
$code =~ s/3/ord(3)/e;
print $code;
$code="Thhis is howw we do itt";
$code =~ tr/a-zA-z/a-zA-Z/s;
print $code;
```

Exit the debugger by executing the following Perl statement:

```
q
```

Getting the Nth occurrence of a match

In some cases, you will want to find the Nth occurrence of a match. In these cases, use pattern matching with the **g** modifier in a **while** loop:

```
#!perl
#1_nth.pl

$line="Code: A127Z Code: B999E Code: G678T Code: T765J";

while ($line =~ /(Code: [A-Z][0-9]{3}[A-Z])/g) {
    $count++;
    print "The $count match is $1\n";
}
```

Try it!

Perform the following steps:

Execute the previous program (1_nth.pl), and observe the output.

Modify 1_nth.pl by taking out the "g" modifier.

Execute 1_nth.pl again, and observe the output (you can stop the program with control-c)

Greedy vs. non-greedy matches

By default, Perl patterns are "greedy". This means that when matching a pattern, Perl will attempt to "grab" as many characters that will possibly match:

```
DB<1> $line="It was the best of times; it was the worst of times"
DB<2> $line =~ s/the.*times/a very bad year/
DB<3> print $line
It was a very bad year
```

The ".*" matched the string "the best of times; it was the worst of" because that was the most it could possibly match. To make your patterns non-greedy (match the minimal amount), use the "?" after the metacharacter:

```
DB<1> $line="It was the best of times; it was the worst of times"
DB<2> $line =~ s/the.*?times/a very bad year/
DB<2> print $line
It was a very bad year; it was the worst of times
```

You can use the following non-greedy patterns:

*?	{n}?
+?	{n,}?
??	{n,m}?

Regular Expression variables

There are many variables that are set as the result of a pattern match:

Variable	Meaning
$`	String preceding what was last matched
$'	String following what was last matched
$+	Last parens match of last pattern match
$&	Last pattern match
$1..$9	Subpattern matches of last pattern match

What was matched

You can "look back" to what was matched during the last pattern match by looking at the $& variable:

```perl
#!perl
#1_match1.pl

print "Enter a line of text and I will find the first 1 digit number: ";
$line=<STDIN>;

$line =~ m/[0-9]/;

print "The number was $&\n";
```

Before and after what was matched

You can see what was in the string before and after the match by looking at the $` and $' variables:

```perl
#!perl
#1_match2.pl

print "Enter a line of text and I will find the first 1 digit number: ";
$line=<STDIN>;

$line =~ m/[0-9]/;
```

```perl
print "The number was $&\n";
print "Before that number was $`\n";
print "After that number was $'\n";
```

Warning about $&, $`, and $'

These variables are only set if you use them in your program. Unfortunately, if you use any of these variables even once in your program, then every pattern match will generate all of these variables. This could have a performance penalty on your program.

There are two methods available to avoid this problem:

Method #1

As of Perl 5.6, the variable @- contains the offset of the first character that was matched in the pattern. In other words, if we did the following match

```perl
$_="abc123";
m/\d\d/;
```

then $_[0] would be set to the number 3 (meaning the third character in the string, counting from zero, is where the match began). Using this value in conjunction with the **substr** statement allows you to simulate the $&, $`, and $' variables.

Example using @-

```perl
#!perl
#1_match3.pl

print "Enter a line of text and I will find the first 1 digit number: ";
$line=<STDIN>;

$line =~ m/[0-9]/;

print "The number was ", substr($line, $-[0], $+[0] - $-[0]), "\n";
print "Before that number was ", substr($line, 0, $-[0]),"\n";
print "After that number was ", substr($line, $+[0]), "\n";

print "\n\n @- \n\n";
```

Method #2

As of Perl 5.10, the variables ${^PREMATCH}, ${^MATCH}, and ${^POSTMATCH} are created if you use the **p** modifier. If this modifier is not used, then these variables are not generated:

```perl
#!perl
#1_match4.pl

print "Enter a line of text and I will find the first 1 digit number: ";
$line=<STDIN>;

$line =~ m/[0-9]/p;

print "The number was ${^MATCH}\n";
print "Before that number was ${^PREMATCH}\n";
print "After that number was ${^POSTMATCH}\n";
```

Special characters in Regular Expressions

In addition to the classes mentioned previously, there are other special characters allowed within Regular Expressions:

Spec. Char	Meaning
\077	Octal character
\a	Bell character
\c	Control character
\E	End case change
\e	Escape character
\f	Form feed character
\l	Makes the next character lowercase
\L	Makes the following characters lowercase until \E
\n	Newline Character
\Q	Disable metacharacters until \E

(continued)

Spec. Char	Meaning
\r	Return character
\t	Tab character
\u	Makes the next character uppercase
\U	Makes the following characters uppercase until \E
\x1	Match hex character

Try it!

Execute the following command to enter the Perl Debugger environment:

```
perl -d -e "1;"
```

At the debugger prompt, execute the following Perl statements:

```
$code="Code: A*+?Z";
$code="Code: A*+?Z";        #should result in an error
$code="Code: \QA*+?Z";
print $code;
```

Exit the debugger by executing the following Perl statement:

```
q
```

Assertions

Some assertions (such as the ^ and $ characters) have already been introduced. Assertions are used to match certain conditions within a string (such as beginning and end of a line). Commonly used assertions are described in the following table:

Assertion	Meaning
^	Match beginning of line
$	Match end of line
\b	Match a word boundary
\B	Match a non-word boundary
\A	Match only at the beginning of the string (note – this is the same as ^ except when using the **m** modifier)
\Z	Match only at the end of the string or before a newline character at end of the string (note – this is the same as $ except when using the **m** modifier)
\z	Match only at the end of the string
\G	Match only where previous m//g left off (this works only with matching, not substitution or translation)
(?=EXPR)	Look ahead match (positive)
(?!EXPR)	Look ahead match (negative)
(?<=EXPR)	Look behind match (positive)
(?<!EXPR)	Look behind match (negative)

Looking forward and back

The "look forward" and "look back" assertions are useful when you want to be certain that a pattern is found, but you only want to "work with" a portion of the pattern. For example, you want to replace the word "great" with "bad" but only if it isn't the last word in the string. The following will allow this to occur:

```
DB<1> $_="This is a good time to learn Perl"
DB<2> s/good(?=.)/great/
DB<3> print
This is a great time to learn Perl
DB<4> $_="This is good"
DB<5> s/good(?=.)/great/
DB<6> print
This is good
```

Or, suppose we want to replace "A127Z" with "-----" if the string "Code: " does not appear at the prior to "A127Z":

```
DB<1>  $_="Code: A127Z"
DB<2> s/(?<!Code: )A127Z/---/
DB<3> print
Code: A127Z
DB<4> $_="Answer: A127Z"
DB<5> s/(?<!Code: )A127Z/---/
DB<6>  print
Answer: ---
```

Try it!

Execute the following command to enter the Perl Debugger environment:

```
perl -d -e "1;"
```

At the debugger prompt, execute the following Perl statements:

```
$code = "Test: A127Z";
$code =~ s/(?<!Test: )A127Z/---/;
print $code;
$code = "Result: A127Z";
$code =~ s/(?<!Test: )A127Z/---/;
print $code;
```

Exit the debugger by executing the following Perl statement:

```
q
```

Using \G

Recall that using the **g** modifier with matching tells Perl to remember where the last pattern match "left off":

```perl
#!perl
#1_g-1.pl

$line="Code: A127Z Code: B999E Code: G678T Code: T765J";

$line =~ /Code: ([A-Z][0-9]{3}[A-Z])/g;
print "$1\n";    #prints A127Z

$line =~ /Code: ([A-Z][0-9]{3}[A-Z])/g;
print "$1\n";    #prints B999E
```

In situations like this, you may want to have the behavior of the ^ (beginning of variable) assertion, but obviously after the first pattern match, the matching is starting after the beginning of the variable.

To specify "beginning of where the previous match left off", use the **\G** assertion. See the next page for an example.

Example of \G

```perl
#!perl
#1_g-2.pl

$line="Code: A127Z Code: B999E Code: G678T Code: T765J";

$line =~ /Code: ([A-Z][0-9]{3}[A-Z])/g;
print "$1\n";    #prints A127Z

$line =~ /\G Code: ([A-Z][0-9]{3}[A-Z])/g;
print "$1\n";    #prints B999E
```

However, be careful of this as a failed match resets back to the beginning of the variable:

```perl
#!perl
#1_g-3.pl

$line="Code: A127Z Code: B999E Code: G678T Code: T765J";
```

29

```
$line =~ /Code: ([A-Z][0-9]{3}[A-Z])/g;
print "$1\n";    #prints A127Z

$line =~ /\GCode: ([A-Z][0-9]{3}[A-Z])/g;
print "$1\n";    #prints A127Z
```

Try it!

Perform the following steps:

  Execute 1_g-1.pl and observe the results.

  Execute 1_g-2.pl and observer the results.

  Execute 1_g-3.pl and observer the results.

Reading from filehandles using `split`

In the *Beginning Perl Programming: From Novice to Professional* book, the **split**
command was introduced. It was used in that book to break up a string using Regular
Expressions and store the resulting items into an array:

```
DB<1> $line="Bob:Sue:Steve:Nick:Trevor"
DB<2> @names=split(/:/, $line)
DB<3> print $names[0]
Bob
```

   The **split** command can also be used to read from a filehandle:

```
#!perl
#1_split.pl

undef $/;  #undefine the input separator variable
@words=split (/\s+/, <STDIN>);

print "First word: $words[0]\n";
print "Last word: $words[$#words]\n";
print "Number of words ", $#words+1, "\n";
```

Multiple line matching

In cases in which a string contains multiple lines (text separated with newline characters), the behavior of Perl's RE may not be what you want. The default behavior of Perl is to "ignore" newline characters when it comes to matching the end of a string:

```
DB<1> $_="Today is the day\n"
DB<2> if (/day$/) {print "yes"}
yes
```

You can look for a newline character if you want to:

```
DB<1> $_="Today is the day\n"
DB<2> if (/day\n$/) {print "yes"}
yes
```

But what if you want to look for something that appears at the "end of a line"? The following will only look for something at the "end of the string":

```
DB<1> $_="This is a good day\nto learn Perl"
DB<2> if (/Perl$/) {print "yes"}
yes
DB<3> if (/day$/) {print "yes"}
```

You could say "match something followed by a newline character", but that won't match the last line the string unless there is a newline character:

```
DB<1> $_="This is a good day\nto learn Perl"
DB<2> if (/Perl\n/) {print "yes"}
DB<3> if (/day\n/) {print "yes"}
yes
```

To match the end of a line or the end of the string, use the m modifier:

```
DB<1> $_="This is a good day\nto learn Perl"
DB<2> if (/Perl$/m) {print "yes"}
yes
DB<3> if (/day$/m) {print "yes"}
yes
```

The meaning of "$" changes with the **m** modifier. Instead of meaning "end of the string", it means "end of the string or prior to a newline character".

Using the s modifier

Another method that you can use is the **s** modifier. With this modifier, Perl treats newlines just like normal characters. This means that the "." metacharacter will match a newline character:

```
DB<1> $_="This is a good day\nto learn Perl"
DB<2> if (/day.to/) {print "yes"}
DB<3> if (/day.to/s) {print "yes"}
yes
```

Try it!

Execute the following command to enter the Perl Debugger environment:

```
perl -d -e "1;"
```

At the debugger prompt, execute the following Perl statements:

```
$code = "Test: A127Z";
$code =~ s/(?<!Test: )A127Z/---/;
print $code;
$code = "Result: A127Z";
$code =~ s/(?<!Test: )A127Z/---/;
print $code;
```

Exit the debugger by executing the following Perl statement:

```
q
```

Using the \A, \Z, and \z assertions

When you use the **m** modifier, the $ assertion matches "the end of any line in the variable or the end of the string". Additionally, the ^ assertion matches "the beginning of any line in the variable or the beginning of the string".

In these cases, you can still match "the beginning of the string" by using the **\A** assertion. You can also match "the end of the string" by using the **\Z** assertion.

The **\z** assertion will also match only the end of the string but differs from **\Z** in that it won't match if there is a newline character at the end of the string (unless that newline character is specifically included in the pattern).

Commenting Regular Expressions

While you can place comments before and after your Regular Expressions, sometimes it would be nice to place comments within your Regular Expressions to help explain what the expression does. With the **x** modifier, you can place comments and whitespace within your Regular Expressions.

When the **x** modifier is used, comments (# to end of line) and whitespace (tabs, spaces, newlines, etc.) are completely ignored. This means if you want to "look for" one of these characters, you need to escape them with a backslash.

An example of commenting within a pattern:

```perl
#!perl
#1_comm.pl

$_='Code: 127 -- \State=99\ ?UNSET?';

m/
  (?<=Code:)        #Look back for "Code:" but don't replace
  (\ \d{3})           #match and group " " followed by three numbers
  \ --\              #match " -- "
  \\State=           #match "\State="
  (\d+)              #match and group one or more digits
/x;

print "First number: $1\n";
print "Second number: $2\n";
```

Alternative delimiters

Consider the following code:

```perl
#!perl
#1_alt1.pl

$_="Path: perl";

m/\/([a-z]+)\/([a-z]+)/;

print "$1\n$2\n";
```

While it works just fine, the RE can be difficult to read. The problem is that in order to match a "/", you need to escape it.

While most programmers use "/" by default as a delimiter, you can choose any character you wish. If you use a different character, then you don't have to escape the "/" character:

```perl
#!perl
#1_alt2.pl

$_="Path: perl";

m,/([a-z]+)/([a-z]+),;

print "$1\n$2\n";
```

Note   Be careful of what character you choose for the alternative delimiter. Avoid using metacharacters as you won't be able to use that character as a metacharacter within the RE.

Additional resources

In each chapter, resources are provided to provide the learner with a source for more information. These resources may include downloadable source code or links to other books or articles that will provide you more information about the topic at hand.

Resources for this chapter can be found here:
`https://github.com/Apress/pro-perl-programming`

Lab exercises

Mini lab:

Write a program that takes a valid date and converts into this format:

January 01, 2001

The format of the valid date should be `"01/01/2001"`. The first number should be between 01 and 12. The second number should be between 01 and 31. The last number should be a four-digit number.

Don't worry about `"errors"` such as `"02/31/2001"`.

If an incorrect date is given, display an error message and ask for the input again.

Primary lab:

> A note about the lab exercises in this book: Creating lab exercises that will be beneficial to all learners can be difficult. Lab exercises that focus on specific scenarios (such as engineering test cases) can result in difficulties for learners who do not perform this sort of programming. As a result, the focus of these labs is to perform tasks that are fairly generic, but that also assist the learners in practicing the new skills that are learned in this book. In addition, to make the lab exercises more realistic, you will build on one primary script throughout the book rather than build many, small scripts.

Throughout this book you will be creating one script. The script will take the output provided by a Perl script and parse the data. For this unit you will do the following:

When your script begins, open a file handle to read the output of the data.pl program. Read the data, perform Regular Expression substitution listed below, and assign this data to an array:

- Remove all leading whitespace in each element.

- Compress all multiple spaces into a single space.

Create a main menu that has the following options (you will add more options as the book progresses):

1. Remove newline characters from each element.

2. Convert dates into 01/31 format.

3. Remove PPID field.

4. Print the array.

5. Exit.

Write the code for each of the preceding options.
Notes and hints:

- If you don't remember how to open a file handle that reads the output of an OS command, review the lab1-hints.txt file.

- When printing the array, consider sending the data to the OS command "more".

- If the user runs option #3 more than one time, nothing should happen after the first time.

- Use subroutines to logically break up your program.

When you have completed your work, compare your script against the parse1.pl file provided in lab answers.

CHAPTER 2

Advanced Regular Expressions

So, you think you know a lot about Perl Regular Expressions? If you finished Chapter 1, then you certainly do. But, there are more REs that provide you with powerful techniques to parse data.

This chapter covered REs that will give you a great understanding of how useful Perl pattern matching is. Each section in this chapter will also start with a brief description why you should learn that technique.

Make use of the Smartmatch operator

Why   This operator provides a more powerful technique to perform matching.

The Smartmatch operator, **~~**, will perform matching of items based on their context. In other words, it behaves differently (polymorphic) depending on the values being compared. It returns true (1) if the match is made and false ("") if the match is not made.

Consider how you currently look for a key in a hash:

```
if ( exists $hash{key} ) { }
```

This could also be done with smart matching:

```
if ( $key ~~ %hash) { }
```

37

© William "Bo" Rothwell of One Course Source, Inc. 2020
W. "Bo" Rothwell, *Pro Perl Programming*, https://doi.org/10.1007/978-1-4842-5605-3_2

> **Note**   Think of **~~** as "in" or "inside of" when you convert this into a verbal expression. For example, you could think of the previous code as "$key is inside of %hash".

Using REs with Smartmatch

In the preceding example, there wasn't any difference between using **exists** and **~~**. However, what if you wanted to look for a key based on a regular expression?

```
if (%hash ~~ /^A/) {
    print "A key that started with A was found\n";
}
```

The same could be done with an array (although **grep** would have done the trick as well, just not as fast as **~~**):

```
if (@array ~~ /^A/) {
    print "A element that started with A was found\n";
}
```

> **Note**   Due to how the Smartmatch operator works, the order of the parameters doesn't matter. In other words, **@array ~~ /^A/** is the same as **/^A/ ~~ @array**.

Additional Smartmatches

You can use Smartmaches to perform other sorts of matching. For example, to find if two arrays have the same elements in the same order:

```
if (@array1 ~~ @array2) { }
```

To see if all of the keys of one hash are the same as another hash:

```
if (%hash1 ~~ %hash2) { }
```

Suppose you had a list of scalars in an array and you want to determine if one of those is a key within a hash:

```
if (%hash ~~ @array) { }
```

The given statement

> **Note**   You may wonder why references are made to previous versions of Perl 5. The author believes it is important to know when new features were added when dealing with legacy code. This could explain why a bit of legacy code doesn't use a newer, more effective Perl feature.

Smartmatching is often used with the **given** statement, a feature introduced in Perl 5.10. The **given** statement is a feature that will be available in Perl 6 and has been "backported" to Perl 5. To make use of a new feature in Perl 5, use the following syntax:

```
#!perl
#given1.pl

use feature "switch";  #Provides access to the given statement

print "Please enter 'yes' or 'no': ";
$response=<STDIN>;
chomp $response;

given ($response) {
        when ("yes") {print "You agree!\n"; }
        when ("no")  {print "Bummer, you don't agree\n"; }
        default    {print "Maybe next time\n"; }
}
```

You can refer to the variable that **given** is "looking in" as **$_**. So, the previous could have been written like this:

```
given ($response) {
        when ($_ eq "yes") {print "You agree!\n"; }
        when ($_ eq "no")  {print "Bummer, you don't agree\n"; }
        default    {print "Maybe next time\n"; }
}
```

So, to use ~~, you can do the following:

```perl
#!perl
#given2.pl

use feature "switch";

print "Please enter 'yes' or 'no': ";
$response=<STDIN>;
chomp $response;

given ($response) {
        when ($_ ~~ /^y/) {print "You agree!\n"; }
        when ($_ ~~ /^n/)  {print "Bummer, you don't agree\n"; }
        default    {print "Maybe next time\n"; }
}
```

What is given's default?

Consider the code from the first given example:

```perl
given ($response) {
        when ("yes") {print "You agree!\n"; }
        when ("no")  {print "Bummer, you don't agree\n"; }
        default    {print "Maybe next time\n"; }
}
```

So, if you don't specify Regular Expression pattern matching, what exactly is **given** doing? That isn't an easy question to answer. Consider what the documentation (see http://perldoc.perl.org/perlsyn.html) states:

> Exactly what the EXPR argument to when does is hard to describe precisely, but in general, it tries to guess what you want done. Sometimes it is interpreted as $_ ~~ EXPR, and sometimes it does not. It also behaves differently when lexically enclosed by a given block than it does when dynamically enclosed by a foreach loop. The rules are far too difficult to understand to be described here. See Experimental Details on given and when later on.

As a result, it might be best to be clear and specific about how you want the match/comparison to be performed.

Use Perl 5.10.1 or higher

Smartmatch was introduced in Perl 5.10. However, it was significantly modified in Perl 5.10.1, so it works differently in 5.10.1 and higher. To make sure your code uses the 5.10.1 version of Smartmatch, make sure the following is in your code:

```
use 5.010001;
```

Understand Regular Expression precedence

Why   Understanding precedence allows you to better understand how pattern matching works.

Understanding the precedence of Regular Expression (regex) operators will allow you to create more concise patterns. There are four levels of regex precedence, from highest to lowest:

Operators	Description
() (?:) etc.	Parentheses/grouping
? + * {m,n} +? ++ etc.	Repetition
^ $ abc \G \b \B [abc]	Sequence/literal characters/character classes
a|b	Alternation

To see an example of how important understanding precedence is, look at the following:

```perl
#!perl
#precedence1.pl

$_="This is simply a test";

if (/^This|test$/) {print "Match 1\n";}
if (/^(This|test)$/) {print "Match 2\n";}
```

```
$_="This";

if (/^This|test$/) {print "Match 3\n";}
if (/^(This|test)$/) {print "Match 4\n";}
```

There is a fundamental difference in the pattern matches with and without the parentheses because the | character has a lower precedence than ^ and $. The following expression means "Match' This' at the beginning of the string or 'test' at the end of the string":

```
if (/^This|test$/) {print "Match 1\n";}
```

With the parentheses, the pattern means "Match the beginning of the string, followed by either' This' or 'test', followed by the end of the string":

```
if (/^(This|test)$/) {print "Match 2\n";}
```

Understand what is *NOT* a Regular Expression atom

Why   Some character sequences appear to be regex patterns when they are in fact string patterns. Knowing this helps you with understanding how pattern matching works.

Consider an atom to be those special characters in a pattern that are interpolated by the Regular Expression engine (*, +, ., ?, etc.). Sometimes Perl programmers feel that some expressions are regex atoms when they are really just string interpolations.

For example, in the following code:

```
$var =~ m/^test\t\U$var\E123$/;
```

the following are not regex atoms: \t, \U, $var, and \E. These are, instead, string characters that are interpolated *before* the regex engine sees that pattern.

In most cases, this isn't an issue, but with variables, you need to be careful as they may contain characters that are later interpolated as regex atoms:

```
$var=<STDIN>;                      #Suppose the user inputs [abc
$var =~ m/^test\t\U$var\E123$/;    #Will result in a run time error.
```

Using Regular Expressions in list context

Why   This technique provides a more clear way of capturing submatches.

At this point, you should know that the following expression will create three variables, **$1**, **$2**, and **$3**:

```
$_="Code: A127Z Code: B999Y Code: Z876G";
m/Code: (\w\d{3}\w) Code: (\w\d{3}\w) Code: (\w\d{3}\w)/;
```

Typically, after the match, you will want to do something like this:

```
$first=$1;
$second=$2;
$third=$3;
```

There are two reasons why reassigning the variables is a "good idea":

1. **$1**, **$2**, and **$3** are not very descriptive names.

2. If another pattern match occurs, either by you or a function that you call, you may lose the values stored in **$1**, **$2**, and **$3** as they will be replaced by values from the new pattern match results.

Instead of making copies of the **$1**, **$2**, and **$3** variables, you can just have the values placed directly into an array by using the regex match in list context. For example:

```
#!perl
#list1.pl

$_="Code: A127Z Code: B999Y Code: Z876G";
@values = m/Code: (\w\d{3}\w) Code: (\w\d{3}\w) Code: (\w\d{3}\w)/;

$"="\n";
print "@values", "\n";
```

Because the return value of the regex match is being used to assign to an array, the return value of the regex match is in list context. For regex matching, list context returns a list of the values matches within the **( )** characters.

Note that the **$1**, **$2**, and **$3** variables are still created but no longer needed.

You can also assign these to scalar variables by placing a list on the left of the assignment operator:

```perl
#!perl
#list2.pl

$_="Code: A127Z Code: B999Y Code: Z876G";
($first, $second, $third) = m/Code: (\w\d{3}\w) Code: (\w\d{3}\w) Code: (\w\d{3}\w)/;

$"="\n";
print "$first\n$second\n$third\n";
```

Naming the capture variables within the pattern match

There is another technique that can provide completely different variable names, bypassing the **$1**, **$2**, and **$3** variable names. As of Perl 5.10, you can use the following syntax:

```perl
#!perl
#list3.pl

$_="Code: A127Z Code: B999Y Code: Z876G";
m/Code: (?<first>\w\d{3}\w) Code: (?<second>\w\d{3}\w) Code: (?<third>\w\d{3}\w)/;

$"="\n";
print "$+{first}\n$+{second}\n$+{third}\n";
```

Instead of placing the captured values in scalar variables, they are placed in the **%+** hash with the key being what was placed within the < > characters.

If you use this technique, you won't have any of the dollar-sign variables (**$1**, **$2**, **$3**, etc.) nor will you have access to the backslash references (**\1**, **\2**, **\3**, etc). Instead, you use the format of **\k<label>** where label is the name of the key.

You can also make use of relative positions of the **\g#** (replace **#** with the numeric location of the capture):

```perl
m/^(?<first>\w\d{3}\w)(?<second>\w\d{3}\w)\g1$/;          #backref first
                                                          match
m/^(?<first>\w\d{3}\w)(?<second>\w\d{3}\w)\g{-1}$/;       #backref -1 back
                                                          match
```

Match whitespace properly

Why   Limitations with **\s** may prompt you to use **"new"** whitespace pattern-matching characters.

The **\s** regex pattern matches any single whitespace character, including **""**, **\t**, **\n**, **\r**, a formfeed character, and other similar characters. While this might seem like a good way to match a whitespace character, consider the following:

```
DB<1> $_="This     needs to be\t\tcut down\nto single     spaces"
DB<2> print
This     needs to be               cut down
to single     spaces
DB<3> s/\s+/ /g
DB<4> print
This needs to be cut down to single spaces
```

In the previous example, the intent was to convert all multiple spaces and tabs into single spaces. However, since **\s** also matches **\n**, the newline character is replaced with a space.

What you really want to do is march all horizontal white space, which as of Perl 5.10 you can do by using the **\h** regex pattern:

```
DB<1> $_="This     needs to be\t\tcut down\nto single     spaces"
DB<2> print
This     needs to be               cut down
to single     spaces
DB<3> s/\h+/ /g
DB<4> print
This needs to be cut down
to single spaces
```

You can also use **\v** to match vertical white space: the carriage return, newline, form feed, vertical tab, and Unicode line and paragraph separators. Additionally, **\H** matches "non-horizontal whitespace characters" and **\V** matches "non-vertical whitespace characters".

Matching "end of the line"

On different systems, lines end with different character(s): a newline character, a return character, a combination of a return and newline characters, Unicode eol, etc. This makes matching the end of any line difficult as it would depend on what system the file was created on.

In Perl 5.10, a new character was introduced to match any **"end-of-line"** character on any system: **\R**.

In Perl 5.12, a new character was introduced to match any single character that isn't a newline character: **\N**. By default, the dot (**.**) character matches any single character except a newline, but this can be modified with the **s** modifier. The **\N** character isn't affected by the **s** modifier.

Use \G

Why   It results in more **"normal"** behavior when matching with the **/g** modifier.

Recall that using the **g** modifier with matching tells Perl to remember where the last pattern match "left off":

```perl
#!perl
#g-1.pl

$line="Code: A127Z Code: B999E Code: G678T Code: T765J";

$line =~ /Code: ([A-Z][0-9]{3}[A-Z])/g;
print "$1\n";    #prints A127Z

$line =~ /Code: ([A-Z][0-9]{3}[A-Z])/g;
print "$1\n";    #prints B999E
```

In situations like this, you may want to use the **^** assertion, but obviously after the first pattern match, nothing will match because the matching has to start at the beginning of the variable.

To specify "beginning of where the previous match left off", use the **\G** assertion:

```
#!perl
#g-2.pl

$line="Code: A127Z Code: B999E Code: G678T Code: T765J";

$line =~ /Code: ([A-Z][0-9]{3}[A-Z])/g;
print "$1\n";   #prints A127Z

$line =~ /\G Code: ([A-Z][0-9]{3}[A-Z])/g;
print "$1\n";    #prints B999E
```

However, be careful of this as a failed match resets back to the beginning of the variable:

```
#!perl
#g-3.pl

$line="Code: A127Z Code: B999E Code: G678T Code: T765J";

$line =~ /Code: ([A-Z][0-9]{3}[A-Z])/g;
print "$1\n";    #prints A127Z

$line =~ /\GCode: ([A-Z][0-9]{3}[A-Z])/g;
print "$1\n";    #prints A127Z
```

Use the \A, \Z, and \z assertions

Why   Allows the **"default"** behavior when using the m modifier.

When you use the **m** modifier, the **$** assertion matches "the end of any line in the variable or the end of the string". Additionally, the **^** assertion matches "the beginning of any line in the variable or the beginning of the string".

In these cases, you can still match "the beginning of the string" by using the **\A** assertion. You can also match "the end of the string" by using the **\Z** assertion.

The **\z** assertion will also match only the end of the string but differs from **\Z** in that it won't match if there is a newline character at the end of the string (unless that newline character is specifically included in the pattern).

For example:

```
DB<1> $_="This is a good\nday to learn Perl\n"
DB<2> print "true" if /^day/m
true
DB<3> print "true" if /\Aday/m

DB<4> print "true" if /^This/m
true
DB<5> print "true" if /\AThis/m
true
DB<6> print "true" if /good$/m
true
DB<7> print "true" if /good\Z/m

DB<8> print "true" if /Perl$/m
true
DB<9> print "true" if /Perl\Z/m
true
DB<10> print "true" if /Perl\z/m
```

Avoid capturing

Why   Sometimes you need grouping, but you don't want the data to be captured.

Grouping is used for several reasons: in order to have a repeating operation occur on a group, to limit the scope of the "or" operation, and to capture what is match.

When you use grouping for the first two reasons listed, it also captures what was matched:

```
#!perl
#group1.pl

$_="Code: 111ABCABCABC999";
```

```perl
if (/111(ABC)+999/) {
   print "$1\n";
 }
```

As you can see from the previous example, there is no point to capturing what was matched. The value that will always be matched is "ABC". If you execute this pattern once, it probably isn't a big deal. But, suppose you were parsing a large file, one line at a time. In that case, you don't want to have Perl create **$1** for each match, so you can use the following:

```perl
#!perl
#group2.pl

$_="Code: 111ABCABCABC999";

if (/111(?:ABC)+999/) {
   print "$1\n";
}
```

The **?:** in the beginning of the parenthesis tells Perl to not store what is matched in a variable.

It is also important to know about this feature when using the **split** command. Consider the following example:

```perl
#!perl
#group3.pl

$_="Bob~Smith:29:manager:San Diego";

@fields = split (/(:|~)/, $_);

$"="\n";
print "@fields","\n";
```

Normally with the **split** command, the "separator" value isn't passed back into the list that **split** generates. But, if you use parentheses like the preceding example, then the output will also include the separators values:

```
ocs% perl group3.pl
Bob
~

Smith
:

29
:

manager
:

San Diego
```

Clearly not what we want. To avoid these extra fields, use the ?: feature:

```
#!perl
#group4.pl

$_="Bob~Smith:29:manager:San Diego";

@fields = split (/(?::|~)/, $_);

$"="\n";
print "@fields","\n";
```

Output:

```
ocs% perl group4.pl
Bob
Smith
29
manager
San Diego
```

Note   If the syntax of **(?::|~)** is confusing because of the repeating colons, consider writing this as **(?:~|:)**.

Avoid the variables $`, $&, and $'

Why   Using any of these variables, even once in your program, can result in a performance penalty in other locations in your program.

These variables are only set if you use them in your program. Unfortunately, if you use any of these variables even once in your program, then every pattern match will generate all of these variables. This could have a performance penalty on your program.

There are two methods available to avoid this problem.

Method #1

As of Perl 5.6, the variable **@-** contains the offset of the first character that was matched in the pattern. In other words, if we did the following match

```
$_="abc123";
m/\d\d/;
```

then **$-[0]** would be set to the number 3 (meaning the third character in the string, counting from zero, is where the match began). Using this value in conjunction with the **substr** statement allows you to simulate the **$&, $`**, and **$'** variables. See the example in the next section.

Example using @-

```
#!perl
#match1.pl

print "Enter a line of text and I will find the first 1 digit number: ";
$line=<STDIN>;

$line =~ m/[0-9]/;

print "The number was ", substr($line, $-[0], $+[0] - $-[0]), "\n";
print "Before that number was ", substr($line, 0, $-[0]),"\n";
print "After that number was ", substr($line, $+[0]), "\n";

print "\n\n @- \n\n";
```

51

Method #2

As of Perl 5.10, the variables **${^PREMATCH}**, **${^MATCH}**, and **${^POSTMATCH}** are created if you use the **p** modifier. If this modifier is not used, then these variables are not generated:

```perl
#!/usr/local/bin/perl
#1_match4.pl

print "Enter a line of text and I will find the first 1 digit number: ";
$line=<STDIN>;

$line =~ m/[0-9]/p;

print "The number was ${^MATCH}\n";
print "Before that number was ${^PREMATCH}\n";
print "After that number was ${^POSTMATCH}\n";
```

Compile your Regular Expressions before using them

Why   Non-compiled regex patterns can result in error or unnecessary operations.

Consider the following code fragment:

```perl
open (GROUP, "</etc/group") || die;
@match=('\d', '\d\d', '\d\d\d');
while (<GROUP>) {
    foreach $pattern (@match) {
        if (/$pattern/) {
            print "$pattern matches $_";
        }
    }
}
```

The great thing about being able to put patterns in variables is that it is easier to maintain your code when you need to perform pattern matching using many different patterns.

The drawback to this technique is how Perl handles the Regular Expression stored in the variable. When the regex is stored in a variable, Perl doesn't compile the regex until run time. When Perl compiles a regex, it determines if the regex is a valid one, and, if so, it generates a "compiled" regex. If the regex isn't valid, Perl will produce an error and exit the execution of the script.

Run time vs. compile time

Consider the following example:

```perl
#!perl
#compile1.pl

open (GROUP, "<group") || die;
while (<GROUP>) {
    if (/\d/) {
        print "$pattern matches $_";
    }
    if (/\d\d/) {
        print "$pattern matches $_";
    }
    if (/\d\d\d**/) {
        print "$pattern matches $_";
    }
}
```

The third pattern match is invalid, which results in a compile time error. Any non-variable regex patterns are compiled during the normal compile time:

```
ocs% compile1.pl
Nested quantifiers before HERE mark in regex m/\d\d\d** << HERE / at
compile1.pl line 12.
```

Compare the following example to the preceding example:

```perl
#!perl
#compile2.pl

open (GROUP, "<group") || die;
@match=('\d', '\d\d', '\d\d\d**');
while (<GROUP>) {
    foreach $pattern (@match) {
        if (/$pattern/) {
            print "$pattern matches $_";
        }
    }
}
```

When executed, a run time error occurs:

```
ocs% compile2.pl
\d matches root::0:root
Nested quantifiers before HERE mark in regex m/\d\d\d** << HERE / at
compile2.pl line 8, <GROUP> line 1.
```

Why is this a disadvantage? Consider how many times each regex is compiled in this example: three times for every line in the file. For a 50-line file, that means 150 regex compiles (3 REs *50 lines). Imagine if there were 20 regex patterns and 10,000 lines!

To avoid this problem, there is a technique which we can use to store an interpolated regex in a variable: the **qr** function. The **qr** function returns its argument as an interpolated regex:

```perl
#!perl
#compile3.pl

open (GROUP, "<group") || die;
@match=(qr /\d/, qr /\d\d/, qr /\d\d\d**/);
while (<GROUP>) {
    foreach $pattern (@match) {
        if (/$pattern/) {
```

```
        print "$pattern matches $_";
    }
  }
}
```

Since the patterns are being used as REs, the resulting error is a compile time error:

ocs% **compile3.pl**

*Nested quantifiers before HERE mark in regex m/\d\d\d** << HERE / at compile3.pl line 5.*

The best part is that when the variable is used in a pattern, it doesn't have to be "reinterpolated", making execution time much quicker.

Using `qr` to test user input

Consider the following code:

```
#!perl
#compile4.pl

print "Enter the pattern: ";
$pattern=<STDIN>;
chomp $pattern;

$info="Bob:Smith:manager:sales";

if ($info =~ /$pattern/) {print "match made\n";}
```

The problem with this scenario is that if the user provided a "bad pattern", then your program would crash with a run time error:

ocs% **perl compile4.pl**
Enter the pattern: **Bob**
match made

ocs% **perl compile4.pl**
Enter the pattern: **B+***
Nested quantifiers in regex; marked by <-- HERE in m/B+ <-- HERE / at compile4.pl line 10, <STDIN> line 1.*

If you used the **qr** function, it would also result in a run time error and halt your program. But, if you used the **qr** function within an **eval** function, then you could capture any errors and proceed with your program.

Any run time errors that occur within an **eval** call do not cause your script to exit prematurely. They do, however, assign the error message to the **$@** variable which you can use to determine what action to take:

```perl
#!perl
#compile5.pl

print "Enter the pattern: ";
$pattern=<STDIN>;
chomp $pattern;

$info="Bob:Smith:manager:sales";

eval {$pattern = qr/$pattern/;};

if ($@) {
    print "An error occured: $@";
}
else {
    if ($info =~ /$pattern/) {print "match made\n";}
}
```

Using the o modifier

There is another technique you can use to avoid multiple compiles for patterns that contain variables: use the **o** modifier:

```perl
if (/$pattern/o) {}
```

Notes

- You wouldn't want to do something like this for the previous examples because the value of $pattern does change routinely.

- Newer versions of Perl (5.6+) are smart enough to know to only compile the regex if the variable's value has changed since the last compile. Again, this feature of Perl won't be helpful in the previous examples because $pattern does routinely change.

Benchmark your patterns

Why   If you have a pattern that will be used on a large chunk of data, use benchmarking to determine which pattern is more efficient.

Benchmarking is an easy way to determine which patterns will typically run faster. The Perl built-in module **Benchmark** provides several functions, including **timethese()**, which allows you to run similar tests multiple times to determine the speed of each.

For example:

```perl
#!perl
#bench1.pl

use Benchmark qw(timethese);
open (DATA, "<foiadoc.txt") || die;
@data = <DATA>;

timethese(
    1000,
    {
        test1 => q{
            foreach (@data) {
            my ($match) = m/^(\w+) (\w+)/;
            }
        },
        test2 => q{
            foreach (@data) {
            my ($match) = m/^\w+ (\w+)/;
            }
        },
    }
);
```

The following demonstrates the execution of the **bench1.pl** script:

```
ocs% perl bench1.pl
Benchmark: timing 1000 iterations of test1, test2...
    test1: 156 wallclock secs (155.64 usr +  0.00 sys = 155.64 CPU)
    @  6.43/s (n=1000)
    test2: 127 wallclock secs (126.78 usr +  0.00 sys = 126.78 CPU)
    @  7.89/s (n=1000)
```

As you can see, just adding one additional, unnecessary parentheses match can have a significant impact when large chunks of data are parsed.

Use Regexp::Common

Why   Instead of recreating techniques to match patterns that are commonly used, you can utilize the matching tools provided by **Regexp::Common**.

You need to match a variable if it contains a number, so you use the following:

```
if ($value =~ /^\d+$/) {print "yes";}
```

This will match a number perfectly but only if the number is an integer. What if the number could be a floating point number?

```
if ($value =~ /^[0-9.]+$/) {print "yes";}
```

Or, what if the number can have commas for representing thousands separators?

```
if ($value =~ /^[0-9.,]+$/) {print "yes";}
```

What if the number could be either positive or negative? Or if it is represented as an exponential? As you can see, something simple like "match a number" can, in fact, be much more complex than it seems.

The CPAN module **Regexp::Common** provides an easy-to-use technique to match common "things", like numbers:

```
#!perl
#common1.pl

use Regexp::Common;
```

```perl
@values=("123", "123,567", "123.456", "is the answer", "1.23E3");

for (@values) {
    if (/^$RE{num}{real}+^/) {
        print "$_ is a number\n";
    } else {
        print "$_ is not a number\n";
    }
}
```

Output of common1.pl:

```
ocs% perl common1.pl
123 is a number
123,567 is a number
123.456 is a number
is the answer is not a number
1.23E3 is a number
```

The **Regexp::Common** module imports the %RE hash into your program. It is a multidimensional hash that returns complex patterns. There are pre-built patterns that match things like numbers, strings, URLs, comments (from different languages), and more.

You can use **-keep** to store portions of the match as well:

```perl
#!perl
#common2.pl

use Regexp::Common;

$value = "123.456";

if ($value =~ $RE{num}{real}{-keep}) {
    print "$1 is the entire number\n";
    print "$6 is the decimal value\n";
}
```

If you look at the documentation of **Regexp::Common**, you might be frustrated that all of the possible patterns are not listed in the documentation. However, at the bottom of the documentation, there is a mention of where you can find what patterns can be returned by looking at other documentation (**Regexp::Common:number**, e.g., to see possible number patterns).

This further documentation will also tell you things like what exactly **-keep** is doing.

Before you attempt to write a pattern, ask yourself, "Is it likely that this is something that someone has tried to write before?". If the answer is "yes" or "maybe", take a few moments to explore what patterns are available in this module.

The following isn't a complete list but rather an attempt to provide you with some understanding of some of the thousands of possible patterns that are available (note that some of these may require downloading additional modules):

%RE	Description
$RE{num}{oct}	Match octal numbers
$RE{num}{bin}	Match binary numbers
$RE{num}{roman}	Match Roman numbers
$RE{comment}{*lang*}	Matches comments in *lang* (C, C++, Python, PHP, etc.)
$RE{list}{-pat => '\w+'}	Matches a list of words
$RE{list}{-pat => $RE{num}{real}}	Matches a list of numbers
$RE{net}{IPv4}	Matches an IPV4 address
$RE{net}{domain}	Matches a domain name
$RE{zip}{US}{-extended => "yes"}	Matches a US 5+4 zip code
$RE{Email}{Address}	Matches an email address
$RE{CC}{Mastercard}	Matches a valid Mastercard format

If you only want to match subsets of the **Regexp::Common** pattern sets, then load the module this way:

```
use Regexp::Common qw(Email::Address);
```

Take some time to explore other **Regexp::Common** "sub"-modules. For example, there is one that will match different time/date formats and one that will match URLs and IP addresses. There are dozens of them, each providing you with a way to make complex matches easy.

Flags you should consider always using

Why There are flags that affect the default behavior of a pattern, making matches behave more like one would expect.

There are some regex flags that you should consider using by default (note, all three of these were covered in detail in the previous chapter):

Flag	Reason
/s	The dot (**.**) character matches any single character except **\n**. With **/s** the dot character will match a newline character as well, a more natural "standard" behavior.
/m	In variables with multiple lines, you normally want **^** to match the beginning of any line and **$** to match the end of any line. Without **/m**, **^** will only match the beginning of the entire string and **$** will match the end of the entire string.
/x	The **/x** flag allows you to embed comments in regex patterns, which is very useful if you routinely write complex patterns.

Automating /smx

While it is important to use these flags by default, it is a pain to continuously type **/smx** at the end of all of your patterns. There are two methods that you can use to tell Perl to automatically use these flags:

1. Download the **Regexp::Autoflags** module from CPAN and use that module.

2. Make use of the **re** pragma: **use re '/smx';**.

The advantage of the **re** pragma is that you can make any flag a default flag for the program. It is also a standard Perl feature (as of Perl 5.14), so you don't need to download a module from CPAN to use it.

You can also turn off these default flags by using the following: **no re"/smx";**.

Avoid escapes

Why   Using a lot of escapes makes your code difficult to read and understand.

Consider the following example:

```
$var="Code: A.?+*Z";
if ($var =~ /A\.\?\+\*Z/) {print "yes";}
```

Escaping metacharacters often results in confusion, especially since some escaped characters (**\s**, **\d**, **\w**, etc.) have a special meaning of their own. One easy way to "escape" a metacharacter without a backslash character is to make single-character classes:

```
$var="Code: A.?+*Z";
if ($var =~ /A[.][?][+][*]Z/) {print "yes";}
```

Inside of square brackets, a dot is just a dot, a question mark is just a question mark, etc. It may seem a bit of a pain typing, but look at both of the following, and you will likely agree that the second is easier to read:

```
if ($var =~ /A\.\?\+\*Z/) {print "yes";}
if ($var =~ /A[.][?][+][*]Z/) {print "yes";}
```

Obviously this technique won't help matching "unprintable" characters, like the DEL character which is symbolized by the octal value \177. Not only is this confusing to read, but it is hard to memorize all of the special "unprintable" characters' octal values.

A better solution might be to make use of the **charnames** pragma:

```
use charnames qw (:full);
```

Now to match a DEL character, you can use the more human-readable format of **\N{DELETE}**.

Use the **re** pragma

Why   Using the **re** pragma can help you debug your Regular Expression patterns.

The **re** pragma is designed to alter regular expression behavior. In addition to allowing you to specify default flags (see previous section), there are other features that the **re** pragma provides.

use **re** 'debug'

When you enable debug mode, debugging messages are displayed. By default, you see both compile time message (when it generates the regex) and run time messages (when it matches the pattern in a string):

```perl
#!perl
#debug1.pl

use re 'debug';

$var="Code: A127Z";
if ($var =~ m/[A-Z]\d{3}[A-Z]/) {print "yes";}
```

Output of debug1.pl:

```
ocs% perl debug1.pl
Compiling REx "[A-Z]\d{3}[A-Z]"
Final program:
   1: ANYOF[A-Z][] (12)
  12: CURLY {3,3} (15)
  14:   DIGIT (0)
  15: ANYOF[A-Z][] (26)
  26: END (0)
stclass ANYOF[A-Z][] minlen 5
Matching REx "[A-Z]\d{3}[A-Z]" against "Code: A127Z"
Matching stclass ANYOF[A-Z][] against "Code: A" (7 chars)
```

63

```
   0 <> <Code: A127>          |  1:ANYOF[A-Z][](12)
   1 <C> <ode: A127Z>         | 12:CURLY {3,3}(15)
                                    DIGIT can match 0 times out of 3...
                                    failed...
   6 <Code: > <A127Z>         |  1:ANYOF[A-Z][](12)
   7 <Code: A> <127Z>         | 12:CURLY {3,3}(15)
                                    DIGIT can match 3 times out of 3...
  10 <Code: A127> <Z>         | 15:  ANYOF[A-Z][](26)
  11 <Code: A127Z> <>         | 26:  END(0)
Match successful!
yesFreeing REx: "[A-Z]\d{3}[A-Z]"
```

You can also just enable specific debugging output. For example, the following won't display compile time messages (note, "debug" turns on all debugging messages; "Debug" allows you to select which messages to display):

```perl
#!perl
#debug2.pl

use re qw(Debug EXECUTE);

$var="Code: A127Z";
if ($var =~ m/[A-Z]\d{3}[A-Z]/) {print "yes";}
```

Output of debug2.pl:

```
ocs% perl debug2.pl
Matching REx "[A-Z]\d{3}[A-Z]" against "Code: A127Z"
Matching stclass ANYOF[A-Z][] against "Code: A" (7 chars)
   0 <> <Code: A127>          |  1:ANYOF[A-Z][](12)
   1 <C> <ode: A127Z>         | 12:CURLY {3,3}(15)
                                    DIGIT can match 0 times out of 3...
                                    failed...
   6 <Code: > <A127Z>         |  1:ANYOF[A-Z][](12)
   7 <Code: A> <127Z>         | 12:CURLY {3,3}(15)
                                    DIGIT can match 3 times out of 3...
```

```
  10 <Code: A127> <Z>          | 15:  ANYOF[A-Z][](26)
  11 <Code: A127Z> <>          | 26:  END(0)
Match successful!
yes
```

You can also turn on debugging messages for just specific portions on your code as of Perl 5.9.5 because the Debug feature is lexically scoped:

```
#!perl
#debug3.pl

{
use re qw(Debug EXECUTE);

$var="Code: A127Z";
if ($var =~ m/[A-Z]\d{3}[A-Z]/) {print "yes\n";}
}

print "no debugging here\n";

if ($var =~ m/[A-Z]\d{3}[A-Z]/) {print "yes\n";}
```

The **re** pragme can also provide several functions, including the following:

- **is_regexp** – Returns true if value is a compiled regex.

- **regexp_pattern** – Returns a two element list from a complied regex; the first element is the pattern, and the second element is the modifiers.

```
#!perl
#debug4.pl

use re qw(is_regexp regexp_pattern);

$match=qr/^\d+/smx;

#Check to see if a variable contains a compiled pattern:
if (is_regexp($match)) {
    print "\$match is a compile pattern\n";
}
```

```
#Return the actual pattern and modifiers
($pattern, $mods) = regexp_pattern($match);
print "$pattern\t\t$mods\n";
```

Understand backtracking

Why   Understanding how backtracking works allows you to better understand
how Regular Expression pattern matching works.

Consider the following:

```
DB<1> $_="aaaa"
DB<2> if (/a+a/) {print "yes";}
yes
```

When you first learn about Perl pattern matching, you learn that Perl matches from
left to right and that Perl is "greedy" by default. Based on this information, you might
conclude that the previous example should not match.

This conclusion is based on the following logic: **If Perl is greedy, then a+ should
have matched ALL of the "a" characters, leaving nothing left for the final "a"
character in the pattern to match.**

This is sound logic, and the conclusion is true: a+ does (initially) match all of the "a"
characters in the **$_** string. But then backtracking kicks in.

Backtracking allows those greedy patterns to "give back" characters in order to
make the match successful. Essentially, the logic is "a+ could match all of the 'a'
characters, but if it did, then the entire match would fail. So, a+ is
'nice' and gives back one 'a' character to make the match succeed."

It is possible to tell Perl to not backtrack. This can be done by using (**?>pattern**)

```
DB<1> $_="aaaa"
DB<2> if (/(?>a+)a/) {print "yes";}
```

Note that you could also use a++ instead of (?<a+). Here are some other commonly used "non-backtracking" patterns:

Quantifer Form	Bracketing Form
a*+	(?>a*)
a++	(?>a+)
a?+	(?>a?)
a{min,max}+	(?>a{min,max})

Additional resources

In each chapter, resources are provided to provide the learner with a source for more information. These resources may include downloadable source code or links to other books or articles that will provide you more information about the topic at hand.

Resources for this chapter can be found here:

https://github.com/Apress/pro-perl-programming

Lab exercises

Note   There are no exercises for this chapter.

CHAPTER 3

Advanced Features

Consider this chapter a collection of useful advanced tips to help you create better Perl programs. Each section will begin with a brief description of why you should use the feature or tool, followed by more detailed examples.

Use my iterator variables with for loops

Why   This technique makes it clear that the iterator variable is scoped, that is, not available outside of the for loop. It also prevents subroutine calls from accidently modifying your iterator variable, and it prevents compile time error messages while using the strict pragma.

Consider the following code:

```
$name="test";

foreach $name (@INC) {
    print "$name\n";
}

print "$name\n";
```

The final **print** statement should display "test" as the $name variable in the **foreach** loop is automatically localized with the **local** statement. This is generally considered a "bad thing" for three reasons:

1. It is not clear to other programmers (or, perhaps, even yourself) that the iterator variable is localized. By declaring the variable in the **foreach** loop as a **my** variable, the scope of the variable is much more clear.

© William "Bo" Rothwell of One Course Source, Inc. 2020
W. "Bo" Rothwell, *Pro Perl Programming*, https://doi.org/10.1007/978-1-4842-5605-3_3

2. Since the iterator variable is automatically declared with the **local** statement, any subroutine call can access/modify this variable (see next subsection for an example of this).

3. Using "use strict 'vars';" will result in a compile error because **local** variables are not permitted.

Foreach loops use local variable by default

By default, when you create a **foreach** loop, the assignment variable is created as a local variable:

```
foreach $var (@colors) {print "$var\n";}
```

In the preceding example, $var is local to the **foreach** statement. In most cases, this is fine. In fact, it can even be useful:

```
#!/usr/local/bin/perl
#foreach1.pl

sub printit {
    print "$var\n";
}

@colors=qw(red blue green);

foreach $var (@colors) {
    &printit;
}
```

However, this can also cause problems:

```
#!/usr/local/bin/perl
#foreach2.pl

sub changeit {
    $var="brown";
}

@colors=qw(red blue green);
```

```perl
foreach $var (@colors) {
    &changeit;
}
print "@colors","\n";
```

Output of foreach2.pl:

```
ocs% foreach2.pl
brown brown brown
```

You can have your assignment variable in a **foreach** loop be a **my** variable instead:

```perl
#!/usr/local/bin/perl
#foreach3.pl

sub changeit {
    $var="brown";
}

@colors=qw(red blue green);

foreach my $var (@colors) {
    &changeit;
}
print "@colors","\n";
```

Output of foreach3.pl:

```
ocs% foreach3.pl
red blue green
```

Note   This technique can also be applied to **for** loops.

Utilize loop labels

Why   This technique makes it clear when you are using statements like next, last, or redo what loop the statement applies to. Especially useful with loops are long, making it difficult to see what loop the statement applies to.

Typically, labels are used in situations like the following:

```
OUTER:
foreach $name (@INC) {
    INNER:
    while (true) {
        ...
        if (cond1) {last INNER;}
        if (cond2) {last OUTER;}
    }
}
```

For clarity, use a label whenever you use a **last**, **next**, or **redo** statement, not just for nested loops:

```
PARSE:
foreach $name (@INC) {
        ...
        if (cond) {last PARSE;}
}
```

Avoid using <> for file matching

Why   Using <> can cause confusion because the angle brackets can also be used for reading input from a filehandle.

Consider the following code:

```
open (INPUT", "<file.txt");
@data=<INPUT>;
@names=<*.txt>;
```

This seems pretty clear when shown in this context. The second line is reading from the filehandle, while the third line is returning the filenames that end in .txt.

However, confusion (and errors) can occur with code like the following:

```
$pattern=<*.txt>;
@data=<$pattern>;
```

While you might think that $pattern's value would be treated as a "wildcard" pattern, that isn't what Perl will do. When Perl sees a variable within < >, it will always treat it as a reference to a filehandle. To make sure Perl will do file name matching, use the **glob** statement instead:

```
$pattern=<*.txt>;
@data=glob($pattern);
```

Time::HiRes

Why   The sleep command can only sleep in whole integer values.

The built-in **sleep** command can only sleep in whole integer values, so the following command will pause the program for 0 seconds, not .0.5 seconds as intended:

```
sleep 0.5;
```

Using the **Time::HiRes** module (standard as of Perl 5.8), you can **sleep** for fractions of seconds:

```
use Time::HiRes;
sleep 0.5;
```

This module also provides a more effective function called **usleep** that lets you pause your program with even more accuracy:

```
use Time::HiRes qw(usleep);
usleep 1000_001;    #1000=1 second
```

Contextual::Return

Why   The wantarray function is more limited than Contextual::Return.

Many Perl statements are designed to return different values if they are called in scalar context than if they are called in array context. To do this with your own functions, you can use the **wantarray** statement.

The **wantarray** statement can return one of three values:

- true if function is called in array context

- false if function is called in scalar context

- undef if function return value isn't requested

Syntax of **wantarray**:

```
if (wantarray) {                         #if true, need to return an array
    return (@array);
}
elsif (defined (wantarray)) {            #if true, need to return a scalar
    return ($scalar);
}
else {                                   #don't need to return anything
    return;
}
```

However, the CPAN module **Contextual::Return** allows you more flexibility, as described in its documentation:

```
use Contextual::Return;
use Carp;
```

```perl
sub foo {
        return
            SCALAR { 'thirty-twelve' }
            LIST   { 1,2,3 }

            BOOL { 1 }
            NUM  { 7*6 }
            STR  { 'forty-two' }

            HASHREF  { {name => 'foo', value => 99} }
            ARRAYREF { [3,2,1] }

            GLOBREF  { \*STDOUT }
            CODEREF  { croak "Don't use this result as code!"; }
        ;
}
```

See the following example:

```perl
#!perl
#contextual-return.pl
use Contextual::Return;

sub test {
    return
        SCALAR { 'thirty-twelve' }
        LIST   { 1,2,3 }

        BOOL { 1 }
        NUM  { 7*6 }
        STR  { 'forty-two' }
}

print &test, "\n";
print &test + 5, "\n";
&test && print "yes\n";
@result=&test; print "@result", "\n";
if (&test eq 'forty-two') {print "yes";}
```

Note   More advanced features of **Contextual::Return**, such as hash references, are not covered in this book as they are beyond the scope of the book. Please refer to the documentation on CPAN for more details.

Indirect Filehandles

Why   To avoid issues related to scoping.

Consider the following code fragment:

```
sub test {
    open (FILE, "<data.txt") || die;
    #more code here
}

open (FILE, "<junk.txt") || die;
#more code here
&test;

$var=<FILE>;
```

Hopefully you can see the obvious problem here: the **open** statement in the test subroutine clobbers the **open** statement in the main program. This is easy to see (and avoid) in a small program with just one developer, but in larger programs with multiple developers, this can easily become an issue.

Unfortunately, the solution that developers use to avoid such clobbering for variables won't work here. You can't use **my** on filehandles.

You can use **local**, but that isn't the best solution in most cases. For example, **local** doesn't solve the problem in the following code fragment:

```
sub test {
    open (FILE, "<data.txt") || die;
    #more code here
}
```

```
local open (FILE, "<junk.txt") || die;
#more code here
&test;

$var=<FILE>;
```

For **local** to really solve the problem, it would have to be used in the &test subroutine.

The solution here is to use a feature that has been available since Perl 5.6: indirect filehandles:

```
sub test {
    open my $FILE, "<junk.txt" || die;
    #more code here
}

open my $FILE, "<junk.txt" || die;
#more code here
&test;

$var=<$FILE>;
```

Using this technique, Perl will store the filehandle (technically a filehandle reference) into the scoped variable, $FILE. Since this variable is a **my** variable, the subroutine variable won't clobber the main program variable, and the filehandles won't conflict.

The three-argument technique to the open statement

Why   It makes the code more clear and avoids a (rare) potential error.

As of Perl 5.6, you can use either the two-argument technique or three-argument technique to the **open** statement:

```
open my $FILE, "<junk.txt" || die;
open my $FILE, "<", "junk.txt" || die;
```

77

With the three-argument technique, the second argument is how you want to open the file. By making this a separate argument, it is more clear to read and avoids the following rare potential error:

```
$file=">abc.txt";          #Filename is really called ">abc.txt"
open my $file, ">$file";   #will append to a file called "abc.txt",
                           #not overwrite it as planned
```

Always check the return values of open, close, and when printing to a file

Why   File interaction is one of the most common places where your script should fail. This failure could occur when you open a file, close a file, or try to print to a file.

Consider the following code fragment:

```
open my $FILE, ">", "junk.txt" || die;
print $FILE "output\n";
close $FILE;
```

Typically, developers will only "look at" the return value of the **open** statement, when in fact each **print** statement and **close** statement should be "looked at" as well.

Suppose your program opens a file successfully and then the file's permissions are changed before you close the filehandle. This would cause the **close** function to fail (as it is writing data from the buffer into the file).

Additionally, **print** statements could fail due to memory issues or if you have the autoflush variable "turned on". As a result, you should always check the return value of print (to file) and close statement:

```
open my $FILE, ">", "junk.txt"    || die;
print $FILE "output\n"            || die;
close $FILE                       || die;
```

Close filehandles as soon as possible

Why   Multiple reasons (see the following)

Perl developers know that if they don't close their filehandles, Perl will close them automatically when the program ends (or, if using indirect filehandles, when the **my** variable goes out of scope).

However, this lazy programming style can cause problems, including, but not limited to, the following:

- While the filehandle is still open, it is using memory, potentially a large amount of memory if the data is large.

- If something goes wrong (program crashes), you will lose the data if it isn't saved until the end of the program.

Avoid slurping

Why   Reading I/O one a line-by-line basis is normally more efficient than reading the entire file.

Consider the following code fragment:

```
undef $/;
$data=<>;
$/="\n";

$data =~ s/foo/fee/gms;
print $data;
```

This technique, called slurping, may seem a great way of replacing all "foo" with "fee" in a file, but it also has some performance impact. To begin with, if the data being read is large, then Perl needs to use a great deal of RAM to store the entire file. A better solution in most cases would be to read one line at a time, manipulate the line, and then print the results:

```
while ($data=<>) {
    $data =~ s/foo/fee/gms;
    print $data;
}
```

Note   If you have the need to do multiline pattern matching, then reading the entire file into a single scalar might be the best course of action.

Creatively use the do statement

Why   Using the do statement creatively allows you to create more efficient code.

In the previous example, we undefined the **$/** variable (input separator variable) so we could slurp the entire file into a scalar variable. We had to set it back to a newline character so it wouldn't adversely affect other parts of the program.

However, this technique isn't the best solution in some cases. Consider the following code fragment:

```
sub test {
    undef $/;
    $data=<>;
    $/="\n";
}

$/=":"
&test;
$data=<FH>;
```

In the main program, the **$/** variable was set to a colon character but changed by the &test subroutine to a newline character (the default value in most cases).

One way to solve this potential problem is by localizing the **$/** variable:

```
sub test {
   local $/;
   $data=<>;
}

$/=":"
&test;
$data=<FH>;
```

In this example, **$/** "goes back to" its original value once outside the scope of the subroutine.

Note   The **my** statement can't be applied to the **$/** variable.

This is fine for subroutines, but what if you want to temporarily change **$/** (or any special variable) within the main part of the program? You could create scope with braces:

```
{
local $/;
$data=<>;
}

$data =~ s/foo/fee/gms;
print $data;
```

However, for many developers, this is hard to read. It would be more effective and clearer to use a **do** statement:

```
$data=do { local $/; <>};
```

Use the `slurp()` function

Why   The Perl6::Slurp module provides more power to read from files than bulit-in Perl techniques.

Instead of changing **$/** to slurp files, you can use the **Perl6::Slurp** module from CPAN and use the **slurp** function:

```
use Perl6::Slurp;
$data=slurp <FILE>;
```

The **slurp** function provides a lot of features. For example, it will behave as a "normal" filehandle read when assigned to an array variable:

```
@data=slurp <FILE>;      #reads each line into an element of the array
```

You can also have it automatically chomp the newline character from each line:

```
@data=slurp <FILE>, {chomp => 1};
```

Or replace the newline character with a different character:

```
@data=slurp <FILE>, {chomp => [:]};
```

You can also change the input record separator for the specific **slurp**:

```
@data=slurp <FILE>, {irs => ":"};
```

Unlike the normal input record separator variable, with **slurp** you can specify a regular expression:

```
@data=slurp <FILE>, {irs => qr/:|-/};
```

Test for interactivity

Why   If you have a program that can be run by either interactive (gathering user input) or noninteractive, use IO::Interactive to test for the interactive mode.

Consider the following code fragment:

```
print "Enter the file name: ";
$file=<STDIN>;
```

The prompt provided by the **print** command is great, unless the user runs your program like the following:

```
%ocs> perl test.pl < filedata
```

If your program is run like this, then the prompt makes no sense. You could generate your own technique to test to see if your program is interactive or not, or you could make use of a CPAN module called **IO::Interactive**:

```
use IO::Interactive qw(is_interactive);
if (is_interactive) {
    print "Enter the file name: ";
}
$file=<STDIN>;
```

You could also use the **interactive** function to print a prompt. It only prints to STDOUT if the program is interactive (it discards the print data if the program is not interactive):

```
use IO::Interactive qw(interactive);
print interactive "Enter the file name: ";
$file=<STDIN>;
```

Use IO::Prompt

Why   The IO::Prompt module provides powerful techniques to read input from users.

The **IO::Prompt** module (available on CPAN) provides a function called **prompt** that allows you to capture user input in a much more powerful way:

```
#!perl
#io-prompt.pl
use IO::Prompt;
```

```
$data=prompt "Enter a line: ";
$passwd=prompt "Password: ", -echo => "*";
$passwd=prompt "Password: ", -echo => "";

$charprompt= prompt "Enter your choice [0-9]: ", -onechar;
$charprompt= prompt "Enter your choice [0-9]: ", -onechar,
                    -requires => {"Must be between 0-9" => qr/[0-9]/ };
```

Important note   due to the way this module has been implemented, it will not work on MSWIN-based systems.

Understand where to find documentation

Why   Knowing where to effectively find documentation is critical for Perl developers.

If you are going to be really effective in Perl, you should get in the habit of reviewing documentation on a regular basis.

One way of developing this habit is to look up the documentation of a Perl feature/ function when you first learn about it. For example, when you are introduced to the **sort** function, spend some time reviewing the documentation about that function.

Doing this on a regular basis provides several benefits, including

1. You become more accustomed to looking at documentation which results in you developing the habit of looking at the documentation whenever you have a problem with your code.

2. You often will learn about new, valuable features that you can utilize in your Perl program.

Note   If you really want to purchase Perl books, there is an excellent resource for you here: `http://perldoc.perl.org/perlbook.html`.

Sources of documentation

For core Perl features and functions, you have two primary sources. One source is on the Internet: **perldoc.perl.org**. The second is on your own system: the **perldoc** command.

The **perldoc** command is used to display POD (Plain Old Documentation). POD is how developers document modules. However, in addition to modules, the Perl core documentation is also in POD format.

To see the core Perl documentation, use the following command:

```
ocs% perldoc perl
{output omitted}
```

Included in the output of the preceding command is a list of other documents that you can view, such as the following:

```
ocs% perldoc perlcheat
{output omitted}
```

If you read through the main perl documentation, you will see a bunch of FAQs. The **-q** option to perldoc allows you to search the FAQs using a keyword:

```
ocs% perldoc -q sort
{output omitted}
```

If you want to see a list of all of Perl's functions, view the **perlfunc** document. This is also an excellent way to see a list of what functions are available on the version of Perl that you are currently using:

```
ocs% perldoc perlfunc
{output omitted}
```

To see a specific function's documentation, use the **-f** option:

```
ocs% perldoc -f sort
{output omitted}
```

If you want to see a modules documentation, use the following syntax:

```
ocs% perldoc File::Copy
{output omitted}
```

You can even have **perldoc** tell you where the module is installed by using the **-l** option:

```
ocs% perldoc -l File::Copy
{output omitted}
```

To see the raw code of a module, use the **-m** option:

```
ocs% perldoc -m File::Copy
{output omitted}
```

Understand context

Why   Perl decides how to handle data based on the context in which it is used. Not understanding this will cause problems in your code.

A feature that often plagues both novice and experienced Perl developers is how Perl determines data based on context. While this has been covered to some extent previously, this section is designed to provide you with a summary of how context is determined.

With Perl the primary way context is determined is with operators. In most cases, the question comes down to the following:

- number vs. string
- scalar vs. array vs. list

Number vs. string

While both numbers and strings are both scalar data to Perl, they are sometimes treated differently (depending on how they are used).

When numbers are used in a "string context", they are converted into strings first and then "used". String context includes

- String operators ("." or "x")
- String functions
- String comparison

- Regular expressions

- Assignment to a scalar variable

The method Perl uses to convert numbers to strings is very simple. Essentially, the number is treated as if there were quotes around it. The only time the number is modified is when it contains unnecessary "0"s. They are dropped when the number is used as a string.

Examples:

```
DB<1> print "abc".12345
abc12345
DB<2> print "abc".123.45
abc123.45
DB<3> print "abc".123.4500
abc123.45
```

String to number conversion is a bit more complex. Perl will "look" at the first character of the string and

- If it is a number (0-9), then Perl will continue to look for more numbers. Once it finds a "non-number", it will stop looking and will convert the string into what it has found.

- If it is whitespace (new line, space, tab, etc.), Perl will ignore it and look at the next character.

- If it isn't a number or whitespace, then the string is treated as the value zero (0).

Examples:

```
DB<1> print "123abc"+10
133
DB<2> print "    123abc"+10
133
DB<3> print "abc123" +10
10
DB<4> print "1.45 xyz" + 10
11.45
```

Scalar vs. array vs. list

When you use array data in scalar context, Perl returns the number of elements in the list:

```
DB<1> @colors=qw(red blue green yellow)
DB<2> $number=@colors
DB<3> print $number
```
4

There is a subtle, yet important, difference between arrays and lists. While arrays used in scalar context return the number of elements in the array, lists in scalar context return the last element in the list:

```
DB<1> $number=qw(red blue green yellow)
DB<2> print $number
```
yellow

It is important to realize that almost all operators in Perl are scalar operators. This includes

- String operators ("." or "x")

- Numeric operators (like "+" or "**")

- String or numeric functions

- String or numeric comparisons

- Regular expressions

- Assignment to a scalar variables

Understand the => operator

Why   Understanding the => operator allows you to write easier to understand code.

The => operator is simply a stylized version of the comma operator. However, it allows you to write easier-to-understand code. For example, consider the following two code fragments:

```
%cities=("San Diego", "CA", "Boston", "MA");
%cities=("San Diego" => "CA", "Boston" => "MA");
```

The second example is more readable, as the association between key and value is visually defined with the =>. Even better

```
%cities=(
    "San Diego"    => "CA",
    "Boston"       => "MA"
        );
```

However, you can also use this => operator for other purposes. For example, consider the following:

```
&test("debug", 170, 230);
```

There are problems with passing in arguments in this fashion:

1. It is difficult to tell what the arguments are intended for.

2. It forces the user of the subroutine to pass the arguments in a specific order.

3. It forces the user to pass in ALL of the arguments, even if you consider some of the arguments as "optional".

Instead, you could pass in the arguments in option–argument pairs:

```
&test(-mode, "debug", -min, 170, -max, 230);
```

Of course, it would be more readable if you used the => operator:

```
&test(-mode => "debug", -min => 170, -max => 230);
```

In the test subroutine, you can read the @_ arguments into a hash:

```
%args=@_;  #-mode, -min and -max become keys
```

CHAPTER 3   ADVANCED FEATURES

There are many ways that you can use the **=>** operator. For example, consider the following code fragment:

```
rename "file.txt", "data.txt";
rename "file.txt" => "data.txt";
```

The second line in the preceding example more visually demonstrates the operation.

Understand subroutine calls

Why   There are three different techniques to calling subroutines. Knowing the differences between them will allow you to make the right "call".

Subroutines can be called using three different techniques:

```
&test (1, 2, 3);
test (1, 2, 3);
test 1, 2 3;
```

In many cases, there is no difference between these three methods. However, in some cases, there are important differences:

> **BOTH & and ():** If you want to put your functions after they are called in your program, using the **&** character is a proper ways to call the function:
>
> ```
> #!perl
> #sub1.pl
>
> &hello;     #ok
> hello();    #ok
> hello;      #error
>
> sub hello {
>   print  "hi there\n";
>   }
> ```

Only &: If you choose (or accidently) to name a function the same as a Perl built-in function, this may cause problems. Calling the subroutine with a **&** character will call your function. Calling the subroutine without the **&** character will call the Perl built-in function:

```perl
#!perl
#sub2.pl

sub chop {
  print  "hi there\n";
  }

&chop;        #Runs your chop function
chop();       #Runs built-in chop function
chop;         #Runs built-in chop function
```

Only &: If you want to just provide the name of the subroutine, such as with the **defined()** and **undef()** functions

```perl
#!perl
#sub3.pl

sub test {
  print  "hi there\n";
  }

undef (&test);      #Undefines test subroutine
undef (test() );    #Run time error
undef (test);       #Run time error
```

BOTH & and (): If you want to call a reference to a subroutine, you need to either use **&** or **()**.

Only &: Prototypes will not work if you use the **&** character to call the subroutine.

Only (): Use **()** when you need to be more clear with how the parentheses are to be used. Consider the following statement:

```perl
print (5+6)*8, " is the result";
```

In this case we are trying to print a mathematical operation, (5+6)*8, followed by a string. The result of this **print** statement isn't what we expected:

11

Why 11? To understand this, you need to understand how parentheses are used in Perl. Parentheses have many different meanings in Perl. For example, they are used to create lists, to specify conditional statements, to overcome precedence, and to specify grouping in regular expressions.

In addition to specifying precedence in mathematical expressions, parentheses are also used to specify the parameters that you want to pass into a statement:

```
print ("This is the formal way to type a print statement!");
```

When Perl sees **print (5+6)*8**, it thinks that the result of 5+6 (11) is a parameter to be passed into the **print** statement. To avoid this, just make your **print** statement a little more formal:

```
print ((5+6)*8, " is the result");
```

Summary chart of different techniques to call a function

Situation	Use &	Use ()	Use Neither
If you want to put your functions after they are called in your program	•	•	
If you name a function the same as a Perl built-in function	•		
If you want to just provide the name of the subroutine, such as with the **defined()** and **undef()** functions	•		
If you want to call a reference to a subroutine	•	•	
Call a subroutine that is using prototypes		•	•
When you need to be more clear with how the parentheses are to be used		•	

Understand and/or vs. &&/||

Why   The subtle differences between these operators can have an impact on your program. Using the correct operators can make your program more readable and understandable.

There is a subtle, but sometimes important, difference between **or** and **||** (as well as **and** vs. **&&**). In many cases they will produce the same results; however, **or** and **and** have a lower precedence than **||** and **&&**.

Consider the following code:

```
DB<1> $test="abc"
DB<2> $new = $junk or $test
DB<3> print $new
```

The intent was to assign $new to $junk IF the $junk variable was defined. If it was not defined, then we wanted $new to be assigned to $test. However, since **or** has a lower precedence than the assignment operation, the way this statement really executed was

```
DB<2> ($new = $junk) or $test
```

The correct way to handle this would be to use **||**:

```
DB<4> $new = $junk || $test
DB<5> print $new
abc
```

Consider the following code:

```
DB<1> @info=stat("sub1.pl") || die
DB<2> print "@info"
1
```

Our intention was to run the **stat** function, and, if it failed to return the data needed from the "sub1.pl" file, use the **die** statement to exit the program. Unfortunately, we end up with the wrong data stored in @info if the **stat** function succeeds.

Because of precedence, what is really happening here is this:

```
DB<1> @info= (stat("sub1.pl") || die)
```

93

If the **stat** function is successful, then the resulting "rvalue" is 1 for "true" because one of the two statements returned true, making the entire statement true. If you use **or** instead of **||**, you will get the correct results:

```
DB<3> @info=stat("sub1.pl") or die
DB<4> print "@info"
2 0 33206 1 0 0 2 119 1355943060 1355943094 1355943060
```

Use Perl::Tidy

Why   There are perl modules which provide you with automated techniques to make your code look and perform better. Perl::Tidy is one of these.

Writing code that has a persistent style can be difficult. The **Perl::Tidy** module (available from CPAN) provides you with a command-line utility called **perltidy** that will take "ugly"-looking code and convert it to "nice"-looking code. Consider the following example:

```
#!perl
#ugly1.pl

my $lines  = 0; # checksum: #lines
my $bytes  = 0; # checksum: #bytes
my $sum  = 0; # checksum: system V sum
my $patchdata = 0; # saw patch data
my $pos  = 0; # start of patch data
my $endkit = 0; # saw end of kit
my $fail  = 0; # failed
```

If you want to line up all of the comments, = characters, etc., then you can run **perltidy** on the ugly1.pl file:

```
ocs% perltidy ugly1.pl
```

The result of the **perltidy** command is a file with the same name as the original but with an extension of .tdy:

```
ocs% more ugly1.pl.tdy
#!perl
#ugly1.pl

my $lines          = 0;     # checksum: #lines
my $bytes          = 0;     # checksum: #bytes
my $sum            = 0;     # checksum: system V sum
my $patchdata      = 0;     # saw patch data
my $pos            = 0;     # start of patch data
my $endkit         = 0;     # saw end of kit
my $fail           = 0;     # failed
```

The **perltidy** command makes many format changes. See the following files for additional examples: ugly2.pl, ugly3.pl, ugly4.pl, and ugly5.pl.

There are also many options to **perltidy** that can change how it formats your code. For example, use the **-i** option to specify how many spaces to indent:

```
ocs% perltidy -i=4 ugly5.pl
```

Or use the **-st** option to have the output go to STDOUT instead of a file.

If you find yourself using the same options repeatedly, you can make them defaults for your account by creating a **.perltidyrc** file. An easy way to create this file is to use the **-dump-options** option:

```
ocs% perltidy -i=4 -dump-options
```

Note   On Windows-based systems, the file name that you should create is **perltidy.ini**. The **-dump-options** option will not create this file automatically, as specified by perltidy's man page:

Under Windows, perltidy will also search for a configuration
file named perltidy.ini since Windows does not allow files with
a leading period (.). Use perltidy -dpro to see the possible
locations for your system. An example might be C:\Documents
and Settings\All Users\perltidy.ini.

The **perltidy** command has many, many more features that you should explore if you are going to make use of it. The documentation for the command is located here: `http://perltidy.sourceforge.net/perltidy.html`.

Use Perl::Critic

Why   There are perl modules which provide you with automated techniques to make your code look and perform better. `Perl::Critic` is one of these.

As its documentation states, "**Perl::Critic** `critiques Perl source code for best-practices`". It is designed to give you suggestions on possible better ways of doing something, which is important in a language that prides itself on being able to do things in more than one way.

In fact, the slogan of **Perl::Critic** is "`Some Ways Are Better Than Others`".

Perl::Critic (available on CPAN) uses "`policies`", rules about how code should be written. These policies come from several sources, including Damian Conway's book, *Perl Best Practices*. Additional policies can also be downloaded.

When it executes, the **perlcritic** command will find any code that breaks the policy rules and reports the code along with a "Severity" level between 1 and 5 (with 5 being the least severe and 1 being the most severe). By default, only level 5 "`warnings`" are reported:

```
ocs% perlcritic critic.pl
Code before strictures are enabled at line 4, column 1.  See page 429 of
PBP.  (Severity: 5)
```

You can make the **perlcritic** command be more restrictive by using the **--severity** option:

```
ocs% perlcritic --severity 1 critic.pl
perltidy had errors!! at line 1, column 1.  See page 33 of PBP.  (Severity: 1)
RCS keywords $Id$ not found at line 1, column 1.  See page 441 of
PBP.  (Severity: 2)
RCS keywords $Revision$, $HeadURL$, $Date$ not found at line 1, column
1.  See page 441 of PBP.  (Severity: 2)
```

RCS keywords $Revision$, $Source$, $Date$ not found at line 1, column 1. See page 441 of PBP. (Severity: 2)
No package-scoped "$VERSION" variable found at line 1, column 1. See page 404 of PBP. (Severity: 2)
Subroutine "test" does not end with "return" at line 4, column 1. See page 197 of PBP. (Severity: 4)
Code before strictures are enabled at line 4, column 1. See page 429 of PBP. (Severity: 5)
·Code before warnings are enabled at line 4, column 1. See page 431 of PBP. (Severity: 4)
Return value of flagged function ignored - print at line 5, column 4. See pages 208,278 of PBP. (Severity: 1)
Useless interpolation of literal string at line 5, column 10. See page 51 of PBP. (Severity: 1)
Found "\N{SPACE}" at the end of the line at line 7, column 1. Don't use whitespace at the end of lines. (Severity: 1)

Obviously, some of these warnings might not be important to you. However, they do provide good suggestions of how you can make your code better overall.

The **Perl::Critic** module and **perlcritic** command have many features. See http://search.cpan.org/~thaljef/Perl-Critic-1.118/lib/Perl/Critic.pm for more examples and features of this tool.

Understand Getopt::Std

Why   If you require data from users, but don't want the script to be interactive, then you can have users pass in data as options. One way to parse this data is by using the Getopt::Std module.

The **Getopt::Std** module is standard in Perl. It provides you with an easy way to parse command-line arguments that are passed in by users:

```
#!perl
#std_opt1.pl
```

```
use Getopt::Std;

getopts('abc');

print "$opt_a\n";
print "$opt_b\n";
print "$opt_c\n";
```

In the previous example, the **getopts** function defined three valid options: -a, -b, and -c. If these options are used, then the argument passed to the options are assigned to $opt_a, $opt_b, or $opt_c:

```
ocs% perl std_opt1.pl -a "test" -c "null
test

null
```

The arguments that are parsed are also stripped off of the **@ARGV** array:

```
ocs% more std_opt2.pl
#!perl
#std_opt2.pl

use Getopt::Std;

getopts('abc');

print "$opt_a\n";
print "$opt_b\n";
print "$opt_c\n";
print "@ARGV\n"
```

```
ocs% perl std_opt2.pl -a "test" -c "null"
test

null
```

You can also have the option/arguments placed into a hash:

```
#!perl
#std_opt3.pl
```

```perl
use Getopt::Std;

getopts('abc', \%ops);

print "$ops{a}\n";
print "$ops{b}\n";
print "$ops{c}\n";
print "@ARGV\n"
```

If you want some options to have arguments and others to be simple booleans, place a ":" character after the options that are to have arguments (the rest will be booleans):

```perl
#!perl
#std_opt4.pl

use Getopt::Std;

getopts('abc:');

print "$opt_a\n";
print "$opt_b\n";
print "$opt_c\n";
print "@ARGV\n"
```

To tell the **getops** function to stop looking at arguments, use a -- option (-- will be removed from the @ARGV array):

```
ocs% perl std_opt4.pl -a -b -- -c "null"
```

If an unknown argument is passed, the **getopts** function will return false:

```
ocs% more std_opt5.pl
#!perl
#std_opt5.pl

use Getopt::Std;

getopts('abc:') || die;

print "$opt_a\n";
print "$opt_b\n";
print "$opt_c\n";
print "@ARGV\n"
```

```
ocs% perl std_opt5.pl -a -b -d
Unknown option: d
Died at std_opt5.pl line 6.
```

Understand Getopt::Long

Why   If you require data from users, but don't want the script to be interactive, then you can have users pass in data as options. One way to parse this data is by using the Getopt::Long module.

The **Getopt::Long** module is standard in Perl. It provides you with more advanced techniques to parsing command-line options than **Getopt::Std**.

Instead of using simple arguments like -a, -b, and -c, with **Getopt::Long**, you use options like --all, --verbose, and --catchall. These options will be easier to remember and will "self-document". Simple example:

```perl
#!perl
#long_opt1.pl

use Getopt::Long;

GetOptions ('verbose' => \$verbose, 'all' => \$all, "catchall" => \$catch);

print "$verbose\n";
print "$all\n";
print "$catch\n";
print "@ARGV\n"
```

One nice feature of the **GetOptions** function is the ability to specify the "opposite" of an option. For example, the following will allow for both a "--verbose" and a "--noverbose" option:

```perl
#!perl
#long_opt2.pl

use Getopt::Long;

GetOptions ('verbose!' => \$verbose, 'all' => \$all, "catchall" => \$catch);
```

```perl
print "$verbose\n";
print "$all\n";
print "$catch\n";
print "@ARGV\n"
```

In the preceding example, the $verbose variable will be assigned a value of 1 if --verbose is provided as an option and a value of 0 if --noverbose is provided.

To pass arguments to options, use the following syntax:

```perl
#!perl
#long_opt3.pl

use Getopt::Long;

GetOptions ('verbose!' => \$verbose, 'all=i' => \$all, "catchall" => \$catch);

print "$verbose\n";
print "$all\n";
print "$catch\n";
print "@ARGV\n"
```

The "i" means that an integer can be passed. For a string, use "s". For a floating point number, use "f".

You can have multiple values passed in by using the following syntax:

```perl
#!perl
#long_opt4.pl

use Getopt::Long;

GetOptions ('verbose!' => \$verbose, 'all=i' => \$all, "catchall=s" =>
\@catch);

print "$verbose\n";
print "$all\n";
print "@catch\n";
print "@ARGV\n"
```

Note that the program would have to be run like this:

```
ocs% perl long_opt4.pl --catch "abc" --catch "xyz"
```

In the following example, you can have users pass key/value pairs to be assigned to a hash:

```perl
#!perl
#long_opt5.pl

use Getopt::Long;

 GetOptions ('verbose!' => \$verbose, 'all=i' => \$all, "catchall=s" =>
 \%catch);

print "$catch{test}\n";
print "$catch{error}\n";
print "@ARGV\n"
```

The syntax on the command line would be

```
ocs% perl long_opt5.pl --catch test="abc" --catch error="xyz"
```

There are other options available when you use **Getopt::Long**. Consult the documentation for further details.

Alternative commenting technique

Why   Commenting multiple lines with # characters is frustrating.

Suppose you had code like the following:

```perl
#!perl
#comment1.pl

print "hello\n";

foreach $var (@INC) {
    print ++$i, "\t$var\n";
}

print "goodbye\n";
```

And you want to comment out the **foreach** loop. To do this correctly, you would have to place a # character in front of three lines:

```
#!perl
#comment2.pl

print "hello\n";

#foreach $var (@INC) {
#   print ++$i, "\t$var\n";
#}

print "goodbye\n";
```

This isn't so bad for three lines, but what if the foreach loop was 30 lines? Or 300 lines?

There is another technique that you can use to temporarily comment out large chunks of code: POD. Plain Old Documentation is typically how you can comment Perl modules with POD.

However, you can also use it to tell Perl to "ignore" lines of code while Perl compiles the code. You do this by turning on POD documentation with "=begin" and turning off POD documentation with "=cut":

```
#!perl
#comment3.pl

print "hello\n";

=begin
foreach $var (@INC) {
   print ++$i, "\t$var\n";
}
=cut

print "goodbye\n";
```

Again, this is meant to be a temporary solution to make it easier to comment out large chunks of code while you are debugging.

Passing notes within a Perl program

Why   If you are trying to `"take notes"` about your program, this technique may be better than using a separate file.

Suppose you are making notes as to what needs to be done in a program. These notes are either for yourself or to let another programmer know some information. Using a separate file (or email) has the disadvantage that this file (or email message) might be lost or overlooked.

You could use traditional comments, but a long chunk of notes would be a pain to comment out. You could use the POD technique mentioned earlier, but that is more designed for commenting out chunks of code temporarily.

Another technique is to place your notes at the bottom of your program after the **__END__** token as shown in the following program:

```
#!perl
#end.pl

print "hello\n";

foreach $var (@INC) {
    print ++$i, "\t$var\n";
}

print "goodbye\n";

__END__
```

You still need to finish the subroutine
that loads the data. Also, you need to make
sure the data file can't be changed.

Anything under the **__END__** token is not considered Perl code. While there are a few features in Perl that make use of this location (such as **main::DATA** and the **AutoLoader** module), this area is rarely ever `"looked at"` by Perl. As a result, it is normally a safe place to place notes without having to comment out a huge section of the program.

Use Smart::Comments

Why   Improves debugging.

Using the CPAN module **Smart::Comments** will help you debug your Perl code by the use of comments. This module will produce helpful debugging messages. Specifically, it looks for any lines that have more than three # characters. Any of those lines will automatically be printed to STDOUT:

```
#!perl
#smart1.pl

use Smart::Comments;

### Acquiring data...
$data = get_data();

### Verifying data...
verify_data($data);

### Assimilating data...
assimilate_data($data);

### Tired now, having a little lie down...
sleep 10;

sub get_data {sleep 5; return "abc";}
sub verify_data {sleep 5; }
sub assimilate_data {sleep 5; }
```

Certainly, this could be done with **print** statements, but **Smart::Comments** has other features. For example, consider the following code:

```
#!perl
#smart2.pl

use Smart::Comments;

### <now> Acquiring data...
$data = get_data();
```

```perl
### Verifying data at <here>...
verify_data($data);

for (1..10) {   ### Progressing...    done
    sleep 1;
}

for (1..10) {   ### Evaluating [===|    ] % done
    sleep 1;
}

sub get_data {sleep 5; return "abc";}
sub verify_data {sleep 5; }
```

Additional resources

In each chapter, resources are provided to provide the learner with a source for more information. These resources may include downloadable source code or links to other books or articles that will provide you more information about the topic at hand.

Resources for this chapter can be found here:

```
https://github.com/Apress/pro-perl-programming
```

Lab exercises

Note   There are no exercises for this chapter.

CHAPTER 4

Advanced Formatted Output

Recall that many people consider Perl to stand for Practical Extraction and Report Language. You may be wondering what part of Perl performs the "Report" functionality. There are several features that provide this functionality as you will see in this chapter.

Review: The format statement

Basic **format** statement features are discussed in the *Beginning Perl Programming: From Novice to Professional* book. The goal of this section is to provide a quick review of what is covered in that book.

If you are already familiar with basic **format** statement usage, then skip to the next section. If not, then you should try the examples demonstrated in this section.

The format statement

Perl provides a method of creating formatted output with the **format** and **write** statements. The **format** statement is used to create a template, while the **write** statement is used to send the output to a filehandle:

```
format FILEHANDLE =
Plain text and placeholder: @>>>>>
$var    #variable values go in placeholder.
```

Notes

- The value of the variable will go in the "placeholder", @>>>>> in the preceding example.

© William "Bo" Rothwell of One Course Source, Inc. 2020
W. "Bo" Rothwell, *Pro Perl Programming*, https://doi.org/10.1007/978-1-4842-5605-3_4

- The FILEHANDLE can either be STDOUT or a filehandle that you create with an **open** statement.

- Each filehandle can only have one format statement because the statements are declared at compile time, not run time.

- The "." (dot) must be on a line by itself. This character indicates the end of the format statement.

After the variables have been set and the filehandle has been opened (if necessary), use the **write** statement to send the output to the filehandle:

write FILEHANDLE;

Placeholders

There are many different types of placeholders that can be use with the format statement:

Placeholder Type	Meaning
@<<<	Left justify text in placeholder
@>>>	Right justify text in placeholder
@|||	Center text in placeholder
@##.##	Numeric output (lines up decimal place)
^<<<	Left justify, break up over multiple lines if needed
@*	Left justify, multiline output

Notes

- Each placeholder character represents one character of the variable, so "@<<<" means "four characters, left justified".

- If there aren't enough placeholder characters to "fix" all of the variable's characters, the extra variable's characters are truncated. "abced" ➤ @<< would result in "abc".

- The "^" placeholder is useful when a variable needs to be divided among multiple lines.

Example #1 of basic format usage:

This example demonstrates the different placeholder fields (left, right, and center), the multiline placeholder field, and the "breakover multiple-line" placeholder:

```perl
#perl
#form1.pl

format STDOUT =
@||||||||||||
$title
Name: @<<<<<    Age: @<<
$name, $age
code: @>>>>>>>>
$code
Comment: @*
$comment
Keywords:^<<<<<<
         $keywords
         ^<<<<<<
         $keywords
         ^<<<<<<
         $keywords
.

$title="Status Sheet";
$name="bob";    $age=25;  $code="674AR3";
$comment="\nDisplays good tact\nworks hard\nsometimes is late";
$keywords="work    effort    late";

write STDOUT;
```

Output of form1.pl:

```
   Status
Name: bob sm   Age: 25
code:    674AR3
Comment:
Displays good tact
```

```
works hard
sometimes is late
Keywords: work
              effort
              late
```

Example #2 of basic format usage

This example demonstrates how the "breakover multiple-line" placeholder may result in not all of the data being displayed. Notice how the value of "raise" is never displayed (the solution for this problem will be provided in the next section of this chapter):

```
#!perl
#form2.pl

format STDOUT =
Comment: @*
$comment
Keywords: ^<<<<<<
          $keywords
          ^<<<<<<
          $keywords
.

$comment="Displays good tact\nworks hard\nsometimes is late";
$keywords="work effort raise";

write STDOUT;
```

Output of form2.pl:

```
Comment: Displays good tact
works hard
sometimes is late
Keywords: work
          effort
```

Repeating lines

The "^" placeholder character will break up text across multiple lines:

```
format STDOUT =
Keywords:^<<<<<<
        $keywords
        ^<<<<<<
        $keywords
        ^<<<<<<
        $keywords
.
```

Unfortunately, this method is cumbersome and sometimes will produce undesirable results. For example, what if the variable $keywords is declared like this:

```
$keywords="work    effort    late    raise";
```

The word "raise" would never be printed.

To say, "repeat this line over and over until the variable is empty", use the ~~ characters at the beginning of the line:

```
format STDOUT =
Keywords:^<<<<<<
        $keywords
~~      ^<<<<<<
        $keyword
.
```

Example of repeating lines:

```
#!perl
#form3.pl

format STDOUT =
Keywords: ^<<<<<<
        $keywords
~~      ^<<<<<<
        $keywords
.
```

111

```
$keywords="work effort late raise";

write STDOUT;
```

Try it!

Perform the following steps:

- Execute `form1.pl` and observe the results.

- View/read `form2.pl` and then execute `form2.pl`; observe the results.

- View/read `form3.pl` and then execute `form3.pl`; observe the results.

Using select

By default, the **print** and **write** statements send its output to STDOUT. You can modify this behavior by using the **select** statement.

```
#!perl
#select.pl

open (LOGFILE, ">data");

print "Starting log\n";  #sends output to STDOUT

select LOGFILE;  #output will now go to file
print "Starting log...\n";
print "No errors found\n";
print "End of log\n";

select STDOUT;

print "End of logging process\n";
```

Using the **select** statement is very useful when you are sending output regularly to a filehandle other than STDOUT.

112

Note   When you use the select statement, it sets the $~ variable to the currently selected filehandle.

Try it!

Perform the following steps:

- Execute `select.pl` and observe the results.

- View the contents of the "`data`" file to confirm that the script wrote to this file.

Warning regarding the select statement

It is a good habit to set the standard filehandle back to STDOUT after you are finished using the "`alternative`" filehandle. This is especially true if you select a different filehandle in a subroutine that others are calling.

If a different filehandle is selected in a subroutine, this can affect the calling program:

```
DB<1> sub sample {select MORE;}
DB<2> &sample
DB<3> print $~

DB<3> print STDOUT $~
MORE
```

Notice how frustrating this can be. A regular **print** statement can't even display the value of **$~** because the output for the **print** statement will now go to another filehandle (MORE in the preceding example).

Advanced **format** statement features

This section focuses on some of the more advanced **format** statement features. If you are using the **format** statement on a regular basis, you will find these features to be very useful in creating rich reports.

113

Top of form

You can add a header to a **format** statement by using the top-of-form feature. To use this feature, specify a special format template called FILEHANDLE_TOP.

```
format STDOUT_TOP =
Sensitive data: do not duplicate!
.
```

When the statement **write STDOUT** is executed, the output from the STDOUT_TOP is displayed first, followed by the output from the STDOUT format template.

Example of top of form:

```perl
#!perl
#top.pl

format MORE =
Name: @<<<<<<<<<<<<<<<<<
$1
.

format MORE_TOP =
Groups from the group file
.

open (MORE, "|more");
open (GROUP, "<group") || die "could not open group";

while (<GROUP>) {
    m/^(.*?):/;
    write MORE;
}

close MORE;
close GROUP;
```

Try it!

Perform the following steps:

- Execute `top.pl` and observe the results. Note: the top.pl program makes use of a provided system file: the group file. This is just a copy of the /etc/group file from a Linux system.

Format variables

There are some variables that can either be used to modify how format statements work or to display information regarding the format:

Variable	Meaning
$~	Current format name. When you specify the statement **write** without specifying the FILEHANDLE, the value of this variable is used. This variable is typically modified with the **select** statement. $~ is set to STDOUT by default
$^	Current top_of_format name. Like the $~ variable, this is also typically modified by the **select** statement
$%	Current output page number; set to 1 when filehandle is first written to
$=	Number of lines per page; set to 60 by default
$-	Contains the number of lines left in the "page". $- is used when you write to the same filehandle more than once. Perl needs to be informed that it needs to "restart" the "top of page" format. This is done by setting $- to 0 (which also resets the output page number variable)
$^L	The value of this variable will be printed before each "top of page" except for the first page

Note   You need to use the **select** statement for these variables to work.

Example #1 of using format variables:

```perl
#!perl
#vars1.pl

format MORE =
Name: @<<<<<<<<<<<<<<<<
$1
.

format MORE_TOP =
Groups from the group file          page: @<<
$%
.

open (MORE, "|more");
open (GROUP, "<group") || die "could not open group";

select MORE;
$==5;
while (<GROUP>) {
    m/^(.*?):/;
    write;
}

select STDOUT;
```

Notes

- The **vars1.pl** program makes use of a provided system file: the **group** file. This is just a copy of the **/etc/group** file from a Linux system. You could use any file that contains 20 or more lines for this example.

- The output of the **vars1.pl** program may be a bit strange because the **$^L** variable was not set to a newline character. See the next example and the Try it! section for more details.

Example #2 of using format variables:

```perl
#!perl
#vars2.pl

format MORE =
Name: @<<<<<<<<<<<<<<<<
$1
.

format MORE_TOP =
Groups from the group file          page: @<<
$%
.

open (MORE, "|more") || die "could not open more";
open (GROUP, "<group") || die "could not open group";

select MORE;
$==5;
while (<GROUP>) {
    m/^(.*?):/;
    write;
}
close GROUP;
close MORE;

print "\n\n\n\n\n";

open (MORE, "|more");
select MORE;

$^L="\n";
$==5;
$-=0;
open (GROUP, "</etc/group") || die "could not open group";
while (<GROUP>) {
    m/^(.*?):/;
    write;
}
```

```
close GROUP;
close MORE;
```

Try it!

Perform the following steps:

- Execute vars1.pl and observe the results. Note that the behavior might be a bit odd (you may need to press the <ENTER> key continuously until the prompt appears again).

- Execute vars2.pl and observe the results. Note that the behavior is better because the $^L variable was set to a newline character, rather than the default formfeed character (which doesn't display nicely on non-printers).

If you plan on modifying these variables on a regular basis, you might consider using the Filehandle module. This module provides methods (AKA, subroutines) that you can use to modify these variables:

```
#!perl
#vars3.pl

use Filehandle;

format MORE =
Name: @<<<<<<<<<<<<<<<<<
$1
.

format MORE_TOP =
Groups from the /etc/group file          page: @<<
$%
.

open (MORE, "|more");
open (GROUP, "<group") || die "could not open group";

select MORE;
```

```
format_lines_per_page MORE 5;
while (<GROUP>) {
    m/^(.*?):/;
    write;
}
```

Note that on the previous page, the "`select MORE;`" statement wasn't necessary for setting the $= `variable`. However, it did allow use to use the write statement without specifying MORE as an argument.

The following methods are provided by the Filehandle module:

- autoflush
- output_field_separator
- output_record_separator
- input_record_separator
- input_line_number
- format_page_number
- format_lines_per_page
- format_lines_left
- format_name
- format_top_name
- format_line_break_characters
- format_formfeed

Padding with zeros

When using numeric fields, you can have the padding of spaces replaced by zeros by placing a 0 as the first character after the @ character:

```
#!perl
#zero.pl

format STDOUT =
Name: @|||||| Age: @<<
$name, $age
```

```
This is a reminder of your appt. on Friday at 10

Please bring @0##.## dollars with you
$amount
.

$name="Bob Smith";
$age=23;
$amount="125.87";

write STDOUT;
```

Output of zero.pl:

```
Name: Bob Sm Age: 23

This is a reminder of your appt. on Friday at 10

Please bring 0125.87 dollars with you
```

Using ^*

The @<<<< placeholder stops reading from the variable once it hits a newline character. If you use the ^* placeholder, it will stop after it hits the newline character, but you can use the ^* placeholder again to continue to read from the variable:

```
Keywords: ^*
          $keywords
~~              ^*
          $keyword
```

printf and sprintf

Both **printf** and **sprintf** are used to generate formatted output similar to the C and C++ **printf** and **sprintf** commands. Both commands accept a format (how to arrange the data) and a list (the data to print).

Important note   Don't use **printf** in cases where a regular **print** command will do.

---

printf and **sprintf** are almost identical. The difference is that **printf** sends its output to a filehandle by default, while **sprintf** returns its output to the calling statement.

Options for `printf` and `sprintf`

Both statements use the following format options:

Option	Meaning
%%	A literal % sign
%c	A character of the corresponding ordinal value
%d	A signed integer (decimal)
%e	A floating-point number (scientific)
%f	A floating-point number (decimal)
%g	A floating-point number (in either %e or %f notation)
%n	The number of chars output in the next variables
%o	An unsigned integer (octal)
%p	Address in hexadecimal (pointer)
%s	A string
%u	An unsigned integer (decimal)
%x	An unsigned integer (hexadecimal)
%E	Like "%e", but using an uppercase "E"
%G	Like "%g", but using an uppercase "G"
%O	Obsolete
%U	Obsolete
%X	Like %x but using uppercase letters

printf and **sprintf** flags

Flags can be used between the % sign and the conversation to modify the output as well. The following chart illustrates these flags:

Flag	Meaning
[space]	Place a space prior to a positive number
+	Place a plus character prior to a positive number
-	Left justify the output within the field
0	Right justify using zeros instead of spaces
#	Place a "o" prior to nonzero octal numbers and a "ox" prior to nonzero hex numbers
[number]	Indicated the minimum field width
.[number]	Results in different behavior for strings, integers, and floats: String – Max length of string Integer – Max width Float – Number of digits after floating point
l	Interpret integers as "long" or "unsigned long" according to the C type
h	Interpret integers as "short" or "unsigned short" according to the C type
V	Interpret integers according to Perl's type

Example: Rounding numbers

The **int** statement will make an integer out of a floating-point number:

```
DB<1> $num=10.75
DB<2> print int($num)
10
```

This method, however, can't be used to round a number. To do this, use **sprintf**:

```
DB<1> $num=10.75
DB<2> $num=sprintf ("%.0f", $num)
DB<3> print $num
11
```

or **printf**:

```
DB<1> $num=10.75
DB<2> printf ("%.0f", $num)
11
```

Example: Modifying numbers

The following will convert an integer into an octal number:

```
DB<1> $num=999
DB<2> printf ("%o", $num)
1747
```

The following will convert an integer into a hex number:

```
DB<1> $num=999
DB<2> printf ("%x", $num)
3e7
```

The following will convert an integer into scientific notation:

```
DB<1> $num=999
DB<2> printf ("%e", $num)
9.990000e+02
```

The following will add "extra" zeros to a floating-point number and add a percent sign after the number and a "+" before it:

```
DB<1> $num=1.9
DB<2> printf ("%+.2f%%", $num)
+1.90%
```

Example: Converting ASCII values

The **printf** statement can be used to convert a decimal ASCII value into its corresponding string value:

```
DB<1> $number=97
DB<2> printf ("%c", $number)
a
```

A faster method, however, is to use Perl's **chr** statement:

DB<1> $number=97
DB<2> print chr($number)
a

You can also convert characters into their corresponding decimal ASCII value with the **ord** statement:

DB<3> $char="g"
DB<4> print ord($char)
103

Try it!

Execute the following command to enter the Perl Debugger environment:

```
perl -d -e "1;"
```

At the debugger prompt, execute the following Perl statements:

```
$num=289.88;
printf("%e", $num);
printf("%x", $num);        #Note, in this case $num is
                           #treated as an integer
printf("%o", $num);        #Note, in this case $num is
                           #treated as an integer
printf("%.1f", $num);
```

Exit the debugger by executing the following Perl statement:

```
q
```

---

print sprintf

In some cases, you may see a Perl programmer use the command **print sprintf**. This isn't any different than using the **printf** statement:

```
DB<1> $num=999
DB<2> printf ("%x", $num)
3e7
DB<3> print sprintf ("%x", $num)
3e7
```

The <> Operator

One of the advantages of the diamond (<>) operator is that it can read from files that are command-line arguments. For example, the following file will parse a line at a time from either STDIN or from the contents of command-line arguments:

```
#!perl
#argv1.pl

print "@ARGV", "\n";

while (<>) {
  $count++ if (/\d/);
#  print "@ARGV", "\n";
}

print "@ARGV", "\n";
print "Number of lines that have at least one digit: $count\n";
```

Since <> reads "multiple files as they were one," it can be difficult to distinguish between different files. In addition, the **@ARGV** array is "wiped out" as a result of reading from <>.

The **$ARGV** variable can help differentiate between different files being read by <>. This variable holds the name of the file that is currently being read.

Example of **$ARGV**

```perl
#!perl
#argv2.pl

$i=0;
@para=@ARGV;

while (<>) {
    if ($para[$i] eq $ARGV) {
        $count++ if (/\d/);
    } else {
        print "$para[$i] has $count lines with at least one digit\n";
        $count=0;
        $count++ if (/\d/);
        $i++;
    }
}

print "$para[$i] has $count lines with at least one digit\n";
```

Notes

- Reading from **<>** will "shift" elements from the **@ARGV** array. That is why @para needed to be created.

- The last **print** statement is to print the output of the last file in the **@ARGV** array.

 Try it!

Perform the following steps:

- Execute the following command: **perl argv2.pl top.pl form1.pl vars1.pl**

- Observe the output of the previous output. Does the logic make sense in the program?

- To better understand what is going on, edit `argv2.pl`, and add the following line right after the while statement:

  print "@ARGV\n";

- Execute the following command: **perl argv2.pl top.pl form1.pl vars1.pl**

- Observe the output, and notice how the `<>` operator removes elements from the @ARGV variable.

Additional resources

In each chapter, resources are provided to provide the learner with a source for more information. These resources may include downloadable source code or links to other books or articles that will provide you more information about the topic at hand.

Resources for this chapter can be found here:

`https://github.com/Apress/pro-perl-programming`

Lab exercises

Mini lab:

Write a program that takes the following user input:

```
First name
Last name
Job Title
Favorite quote
```

Use a format statement to display the user data in the following format:

```
First Name:     Last Name:     Title:
Bob             Smith          Trainer
```

Quote:
    It was the best
    of times; it
    was the worst
    of times.

Primary lab:

Important note   If you did not finish the previous lab, either finish it before starting this lab or use the completed parse1.pl provided in the lab answers folder.

Modify parse1.pl to include the following changes:

- Instead of printing the array with a print statement, use a format statement with the following:

    - Line up each field of data into columns.

    - Print a header for each page of data (each page should be 20 lines of output).

    - Include the current page number in the header.

    - Have the output still go to the **more** command.

Save the file with the name parse2.pl.

Notes and hints

- You will need different format statements depending on what changes have been made to the data.

When you have completed your work, compare your script against the parse2.pl file provided in lab answers.

CHAPTER 5

Exploring Useful Built-in Variables

A good deal of the power and flexibility behind Perl lies in its `"built-in"` variables. Perl's built-in variables provide many functions:

- Allows you to modify the behavior of your Perl script

- Holds important information regarding how your Perl script is running

- Holds data regarding the results of pattern matching

This chapter provides some insight as to how you can use built-in variables. Note that not all variables will be covered in this chapter as some variables are more useful than others and others are a bit more esoteric. Additionally, some of these variables will be covered in other chapters of this book.

Variables reference chart

The following table provides a list of most of Perl's built-in variables, along with a brief description of each:

Variable	Meaning
$`	String preceding what was last matched
$'	String following what was last matched
$+	Last parenthesis match of last pattern match
$&	Last pattern match

(continued)

© William "Bo" Rothwell of One Course Source, Inc. 2020
W. "Bo" Rothwell, *Pro Perl Programming*, https://doi.org/10.1007/978-1-4842-5605-3_5

Variable	Meaning
$*	Multiline matching (depreciated deprecated by the s and m modifiers provided in pattern matching)
$:	Continuation field characters (rarely used, associated with format statements)
$1..$9	Subpattern matches of last pattern match
$~	Name of current report format
$-	Number of lines remaining on page
$!	Current error number or error string
$"	Array separator
$#	Output format for numbers (depreciated)
$$	Process id of Perl script
$%	Current page number of output channel
$=	Page length of output channel
$|	Output buffer flush
$,	Output field separator
$.	Current line number of input file
$/	Input record separator
$;	Subscript separator for multidimensional array emulation
$?	Status of last OS command
$@	Error message from last eval or do
$[	Used to have the first index of an array be 1 instead of 0 (deprecated)
$\	Output record separator for print statement
$]	Version of Perl
$^	Name of current top of page format
$_	Default input variable
$0	Program name

Variable	Meaning
$<	User's real id number
$>	User's effective id number
$(	User's real group id number(s)
$)	User's effective group id number(s)
$^A	Accumulator for write and formline
$^D	Debugging flags
$^E	OS-dependent error data
$^F	Largest system file descriptor
$^H	Current state of syntax checks
$^I	Edit extension passed by -i option
$^L	Formfeed characters for formats
$^M	Emergency memory pool
$^O	OS name
$^P	Internal debugging flag
$^S	Current interpreter state
$^T	The programs start time
$^W	The value of -w option
$^X	Perl interpreter name
$ARGV	Current file name when reading using <>
@ARGV	Command-line arguments
@EXPORT	Methods and symbols the package exports by default
@EXPORT_OK	Methods and symbols the package exports by request
@F	Contains the split of input lines when -a option is used
@INC	List of places to look for Perl modules
@ISA	List of base classes of current package
@_	Argument to the subroutine

(continued)

Variable	Meaning
%ENV	Environment variables passed into script from shell
%EXPORT_TAGS	Names for sets of symbols
%INC	List of where specific Perl modules were found
%SIG	Used to tell Perl how to handle signals

Use English

Many Perl programmers find Perl's variable names somewhat cryptic and difficult to use. To use "nice English names" instead of these cryptic variable names, use the pragma "use English":

```perl
#!perl
#3_eng.pl

use English;

print "Autoflush is set to $| \n";
print "Autoflush is set to $OUTPUT_AUTOFLUSH \n";
```

Important note

While "use English" might be convenient, there is a drawback to it. Consider the following warning from the Perl man pages:

"Due to an unfortunate accident of Perl's implementation, 'use English' imposes a considerable performance penalty on all regular expression matches in a program, regardless of whether they occur in the scope of 'use English'. For that reason, saying 'use English' in libraries is strongly discouraged".

This performance penalty has to do with the Regular Expression variables ($&, $` and $') that were discussed in a previous unit.

Consult Perl documentation for a list of all of the English equivalents.

Status variables

The status variables give data regarding why an error may have occurred. These variables include the following:

Variable	Meaning
$?	Status of last OS command
$!	Current error number or error string
$^E	OS-dependent error data
$@	Error message from last eval or do

The $? variable

This variable hold the status of the last pipe **close**, backtick, or **system** call. This variable will store a nonzero value if an external program fails. If the program succeeds, the value of this variable will be set to 0.

```perl
#!perl
#quest1.pl

$result=`ls -l /junk`;
print "$? \n";   #prints a positive number since command fails

$result=`date`;
print "$? \n";   #prints 0 since command runs successfully
```

Note that the previous example is designed to run on Unix or Linux systems. If you are running Perl on Windows, change the **ls** command to the **dir** command.

The follow example demonstrates that the $? variable is also set by the **system** statement:

```perl
#!perl
#quest2.pl

system "cd /junk";
print "$? \n";   #prints a positive number since command fails
```

```
system "date";
print "$? \n";  #prints 0 since command runs successfully
```

The $? variable is often used in a conditional statement, as demonstrated by the following code fragment:

```
system "cd /junk";
if ($? > 0) {die "cmd failed";}
```

Try it!

Perform the following steps:

- Modify the `quest1.pl` script if necessary for your platform and then execute it, and observe the output.

- Modify the `quest2.pl` script if necessary for your platform and then execute it, and observe the output.

Important note regarding opening pipe file handles

When you open a file for reading and writing, you typically check the result of the **open** statement. For example, the following code fragment will execute the **die** statement if the **open** statement returns a false value:

```
DB<1> open (GROUP, "</etc/group") || die
```

However, when you open a *process* using the **open** statement, **open** will not return "false" if the process cannot be executed. You need to look at the result of the **close** statement or the variable **$?** after the close statement has executed:

```
DB<1> open (PS, "ps -fe|")
DB<2> close PS
DB<3> print $?
0
DB<4> open (PS, "ps -z")
```

```
DB<6> close PS
DB<7> print $?
256
```

Notes

- When you use the **open** statement to open a process, the return value of the **open** statement is the process id.

- You must close the filehandle before you can use the **$?** variable.

The $! variable

This variable reports C library errors. Many of Perl's statements (such as the **open** command) use C library calls to perform their tasks. When a C library fails, the error message is stored in **$!**.

```
#!perl
#bang.pl

open (READ, "</etc/junkfile");

print "$!\n";   #prints error message of lib call
```

The $^E variable

In cases in which the C library calls are further translated into calls to the kernel the **$^E** variable stored the output of kernel errors. Typically, these errors are more verbose than library errors.

```
#!perl
#E.pl

open (READ, "</etc/junkfile");

print "$^E\n";   #prints error message of kernel call
```

Note $^E is the same as $! in many operating systems (Exceptions: VMS, OS/2, and Win32).

Try it!

Perform the following steps:

- Execute the `bang.pl` and observe the output.

- Execute the `E.pl` and observe the output.

The $@ variable

The **$@** variable holds error messages that are generated by failed **eval** statements. Since the **eval** statement isn't covered in this book, the **$@** variable will be discussed in more detail.

Separator variables

Separator variables are used to modify Perl's behavior in regard to handling input and output. These variables include the following:

Variable	Meaning
$/	Input record separator
$"	Array separator
$,	Output field separator
$\	Output record separator for print statement

Input record separator

The "`record separator variable`" stores the character(s) that Perl uses to "`break up`" the data that is read by `<STDIN>`. By default, it is set to a newline character ("`\n`") and, in almost every case, should not be changed. However, there are a couple of situations in which changing this variable can make life a little easier:

Suppose we had a database file which contained a completely flat database:

```
Ted:9930:accounting:Bob:9940:HR:Sue:9950:accounting:
```

In this case, we could change the $/ variable to a colon (":") and read the entire file into an array with each element being a field in the array:

```
$/=":";
@fields=<STDIN>;
chomp (@fields);
$/="\n";
```

Notes

- The **chomp** command actually chomps whatever the **$/** variable is set to.

- It's important to set the **$/** variable back to a newline character as soon as you are finished reading the file.

Array separator variable

When you print an array, all of the elements of the array are displayed "merged together":

```
DB<1> @colors=qw(red blue green purple)
DB<2> print @colors
redbluegreenpurple
```

When you place quotes around the array, each element is separated with a space:

```
DB<1> @colors=qw(red blue green purple)
DB<2> print "@colors"
red blue green purple
```

The **$"** variable stores what character(s) should be used to separate array elements when the array name is place within quotes. By default, this variable is set to a space. To change this behavior, just set the variable to a different character:

```
DB<1> @colors=qw(red blue green purple)
DB<2> $"=":"
DB<3> print "@colors"
red:blue:green:purple
```

Try it!

Execute the following command to enter the Perl Debugger environment:

```
perl -d -e "1;"
```

At the debugger prompt, execute the following Perl statements:

```
@names=qw(Bob Bill Steve Nick);
$"="\n";
print @names;
print "@names";
```

Exit the debugger by executing the following Perl statement:

```
q
```

print separators

The **print** statement doesn't place anything between the items it prints:

DB<1> print ("abc", "123")
abc123

By modifying the **$,** variable, you can tell Perl to place a character between items that are printed:

DB<1> $,=" "
DB<2> print ("abc", "123")
abc 123

This is useful in cases in which you are printing multiple items with one print statement:

DB<1> $,=" "
DB<2> print "The result is", 5+7
The result is 12

138

The **print** statement also doesn't place any characters at the end of the output. By setting the **$** variable, you can have **print** always print characters at the end of each output. For example, to have all **print** statements end with a newline character:

```
DB<1> $\="\n"
DB<2> print "print will now end with a newline char"
print will now end with a newline char

DB<3>
```

Both **$,** and **$** variables are initially not set to any value.

The signal handle variable

Signals are "messages" to your shell program (or any OS process). The most common signals on UNIX and Linux operating systems:

Signal	Meaning
INT	An interrupt signal (^C)
TERM	Signal sent by the **kill** command
KILL	Signal sent by the **kill -9** command
HUP	Signal sent when there is a terminal break (lost connection)
TSTP	A pause signal (^Z)
CONT	A resume signal (**bg %# or fg %#**)

To list all of the possible signals on the system, use the **kill -l** command on a UNIX-based OS:

```
# kill -l
HUP     INT     QUIT    ILL     TRAP    ABRT    EMT     FPE     KILL
SEGV    SYS     PIPE    ALRM    TERM    USR1    USR2    CLD
URG     POLL    STOP    CONT    TTIN    TTOU    VTALRM  PROF
XFSZ    LWP     TSTP    THAW    CANCEL  RTMIN
```

In some cases, you may wish to have your script behave differently when it receives a signal:

1. Errors may occur if a program is abruptly terminated.

2. If your program may not require human interaction.

3. If your program is essential for either the system or software to operate.

To do this, you can modify the **%SIG** hash variable:

```perl
#!perl
#sleep1.pl

sub nostop {
   print "Can't stop this!\n";
}

$SIG{INT}=\&nostop;     #Ignore control-c

print "countdown!\n\n";
$|=1;
for ($i=10;$i>0;$i--) {
   print "$i \r";
   sleep 1;
}
$|=0;
print "Blast off!\n";
```

You can change your **%SIG** hash anywhere in your program. The changes will affect code until you change the hash again. To return to the default action of a signal, set the key to "DEFAULT":

```perl
#!perl
#sleep2.pl

sub nostop {
   print "Can't stop this!\n";
}

$SIG{INT}=\&nostop; #Ignore control-c
```

```perl
print "countdown!\n\n";
$|=1;
for ($i=10;$i>0;$i--) {
    print "$i \r";
    sleep 1;
}

print "Can be stopped now!\n";
$SIG{INT}='DEFAULT';   #Stop script on control-c
sleep 10;
$|=0;
print "Blast off!\n";
```

If you just want your script to ignore a signal, set the key to "IGNORE":

```perl
#!perl
#sleep3.pl

$SIG{INT}='IGNORE'; #Ignore control-c

print "countdown!\n\n";
$|=1;
for ($i=10;$i>0;$i--) {
    print "$i \r";
    sleep 1;
}
$|=0;
print "Blast off!\n";
```

Try it!

Perform the following steps:

1. Execute the following command: `sleep2.pl`.

2. Soon after seeing "`countdown`" appear on the screen, attempt to stop the program by `control-c`.

141

3. Note the message that appears on the screen.

4. Soon after seeing "Can be stopped now!" appear on the screen, attempt to stop the program by control-c.

5. Notice the program ends without printing "Blast off!".

Version of Perl

The version of Perl that is currently running is stored in the **$]** variable:

```
DB<1> print $]
5.00503
```

This variable can be very useful when you want to execute code that will only work in a later version of Perl:

```
DB<1> $var=<STDIN>
This is a test
DB<2> if ($] > 5) {chomp $var} else {chop $var}
```

However, in cases in which you have to have a certain version of Perl, using the **require** statement would be a better solution:

```
#!perl
#req.pl

require 5.6;

print "This is only a test";
```

Output of preceding program:

```
# perl req.pl
Perl 5.6 required--this is only version 5.00503, stopped at ./4_req.pl
line 4.
```

Try it!

Execute the following command to enter the Perl Debugger environment:

`perl -d -e "1;"`

At the debugger prompt, execute the following Perl statements:

`print $];`

`print $^V;   #This is a newer version of the $] variable
introduced in v5.6.0`

Exit the debugger by executing the following Perl statement:

`q`

Program start time

In cases in which you want to see how long your script has been running for, you can compare the current time with the program start time. The current time is returned from the **time** statement, while **$^T** holds the value of the program's start time. Both times are given in seconds from January 1, 1970:

```
DB<1> print $^T
1573589711
DB<2> print time - $^T
12
```

Additional resources

In each chapter, resources are provided to provide the learner with a source for more information. These resources may include downloadable source code or links to other books or articles that will provide you more information about the topic at hand.

Resources for this chapter can be found here:

`https://github.com/Apress/pro-perl-programming`

143

Lab exercises

Modify `parse2.pl` to include the following changes:

- If the `"data.pl"` command fails, have your script exit with an error message.

- Have all of your print statements automatically print a newline character at the end of the string.

- Have your script ignore `control-c` attempts.

- Make sure your script is running Perl 5.0 or higher.

- Use English variable names instead of the regular names.

Save these changes into a file called `parse3.pl`.

When you have completed your work, compare your script against the parse3.pl file provided in lab answers.

CHAPTER 6

Advanced File Handling

File handling is the process of working with data that either originates from an external source (typically a file) or is to be sent to an external destination. Perl offers several features related to file handling that are covered in this chapter.

Review: Basic file handling

Basic Regular Expressions are discussed in the *Beginning Perl Programming: From Novice to Professional* book. The goal of this section is to provide a quick review of what is covered in that book.

If you are already familiar with these Regular Expressions, then skip to the next section. If not, then you should try the examples demonstrated in this section.

Opening and reading from files

To open a file to read from, use the **open** statement:

```
open (HANDLE, "<file_to_open") || die "could not open file";
```

Note   The "<" symbol tells Perl to open the file for reading. This symbol is often omitted as Perl assumes the file is being opened for reading.

Once a file has been opened, you can read from it by using the filehandle. For example, to read a line from the file into the variable $line, do the following:

```
$line=<HANDLE>;
```

The process of closing the filehandle will close the port:

```
close HANDLE;
```

145

© William "Bo" Rothwell of One Course Source, Inc. 2020
W. "Bo" Rothwell, *Pro Perl Programming*, https://doi.org/10.1007/978-1-4842-5605-3_6

Opening and writing to files

To open a file to write to, use the **open** statement:

```
open (HANDLE, ">file_to_open") || die "could not open file";
```

Note   The ">" symbol tells Perl to open the file for writing. If the file already exists, then Perl will overwrite the file contents. To append to the end of the file, use the append symbols: ">>".

Once a file has been opened, you can write to it by using the **print** statement and specifying the filehandle to print to:

```
print HANDLE "First line of text\n";
print HANDLE "Second line of text\n";
```

The process of closing the filehandle will close the port and write all of the output to the file:

```
close HANDLE;
```

Try it!

Execute the following command to enter the Perl Debugger environment:

```
perl -d -e "1;"
```

At the debugger prompt, execute the following Perl statements:

```
open (DATA, ">output.txt") || die;

print DATA "Today is a good day to learn Perl!\n";

close DATA;
```

Exit the debugger by executing the following Perl statement:

```
q
```

Execute the following command to verify the contents of the file you created:

```
more output.txt
```

Piping in Perl

You can open filehandles that take the output of an OS command and send it into your Perl script. Once again, the **open** statement creates the file handle:

```
open (HANDLE, "ps -fe |");
```

Note   The command "`ps -fe`" will run the UNIX command that lists the processes that are running on the system. The "`|`" symbol after the "`ps -fe`" command tells Perl to run the "`ps -fe`" command and then sends this data into the filehandle.

Once the **open** statement has be executed, you can read from it by using the filehandle. For example, to read a line from the output of the command into the variable $line, do the following:

```
$line=<HANDLE>;
```

The process of closing the filehandle will close the port:

```
close HANDLE;
```

Not only can you get the output of OS commands sent into your script, you can also send output from your script into an OS command. For example, suppose you had a large amount of text to display on the screen (more than a screen's worth). You want the user to have the features of the UNIX command "more" to control the display of the text. Here's how:

```
open (HANDLE, "| more");
```

Note   The "`|`" symbol before the "`more`" command tells Perl to send output of the filehandle HANDLE to the UNIX command "`more`".

Once the **open** statement has been executed, you can write to it by using the filehandle. For example, to write the entire contents of an array to the file handle

```
print HANDLE "@array";
```

Note   The "more" command isn't executed until the filehandle is closed. The process of closing the filehandle will close the port and send the data to the OS command:

```
close HANDLE;
```

The following example shows how to take advantage of the UNIX (or DOS) **more** command:

```
#!perl
#more.pl

open (MORE, "| more");

for ($i=1;$i < 100 ; $i++) {
    print MORE "$i\n";
}

close MORE;
```

Displaying the file position

To see where you are in a file, use the **tell** statement. This statement will indicate how far you are from the beginning of the file in bytes.

```
DB<1> open (GROUP, "</etc/group")
DB<2> print tell GROUP
0
DB<3> $line=<GROUP>
DB<4> print tell GROUP
13
```

Moving the file position

To move the position where you are in the file, use the **seek** command. The syntax of the **seek** statement is

```
seek (FILEHANDLE, #_of_bytes_to_move, whence)
```

The whence is where to begin the movement from. The following are allowed:

> 0 – Move from beginning of file
>
> 1 – Move from current position
>
> 2 – Move from end of file

Some examples of seek:

```
DB<1> open (GROUP, "</etc/group")
DB<2> print tell GROUP
0
DB<3> $line=<GROUP>
DB<4> print tell GROUP
13
DB<5> seek (GROUP, 5, 1)
DB<6> print tell GROUP
18
DB<7> seek (GROUP, 0, 0)
DB<8> print tell GROUP
0
DB<9> seek (GROUP, -10, 2)
DB<10> print tell GROUP
281
```

 **Try it!**

Change to the unit four "examples" directory and then execute the following command to enter the Perl Debugger environment:

```
perl -d -e "1;"
```

At the debugger prompt, execute the following Perl statements to practice using the tell and seek statements:

```
open (DATA, "djcdoscommands.txt") || die;

$dummy=<DATA>;

print tell DATA;

seek (DATA, 0, 0)

print tell DATA;

seek (DATA, 0, 2);

print tell DATA;

close DATA;
```

Exit the debugger by executing the following Perl statement:

```
q
```

Opening files for reading and writing

In addition to being able to open a file for reading, writing, and appending, you can open a file for both reading and writing at the same time. The following chart illustrates the reading/writing options:

Option	Meaning
"+<file"	Open an existing file for reading and writing
"+>file"	Create a new file (or overwrite an existing file)
"+>>file"	Open an existing file for appending

Open an existing file for reading and writing

The following is an example of opening a file for both reading and writing (note: the file /tmp/group is a copy of the file /etc/group):

```
DB<1> open (GROUP, "+</tmp/group")
DB<2> $line=<GROUP>
DB<3> print $line
root::0:root
DB<4> seek (GROUP, 0, 0)
DB<5> print GROUP "VOID: Line 1\n"
DB<6> seek (GROUP, 0, 0)
DB<7> $line=<GROUP>
DB<8> print $line
VOID: Line1
DB<9> close GROUP
```

Important notes

- When you open a file using "+<", your position is always at the first byte of the file (position 0).

- Be very careful when printing to this kind of filehandle as you can easily lose data!

- Each character you print to the filehandle will replace one character in the file.

- When you close the file handle, it writes all changes into the file.

Truncating files

If you have a file open for reading and writing, you can "cut off" data with the **truncate** statement:

```
DB<1> open (GROUP, "+</tmp/group")
DB<2> $line=<GROUP>
DB<3> print $line
root::0:root
DB<4> truncate (GROUP, 100)   #truncates all characters beyond 100th
DB<5> close GROUP
```

Why open a file for both reading and writing?

Because the reading from and writing to a filehandle is character-based, you most likely won't find the process of opening a file for both reading and writing very useful. In most cases, it would be better to take the following actions:

1. Open a file for reading.

2. Store all of the lines of the file into an array (one line per element).

3. Close the filehandle.

4. Manipulate the array.

5. Open the file for writing.

6. Print the array to the filehandle.

7. Close the filehandle.

Or, you can edit a file `"in place"` by using the **-i** command-line option (consult Perl documentation to learn more about this method).

While opening a file for both reading and writing is rare, it is important to cover for two reasons:

1. So you understand why you normally don't want to open a file for both reading and writing

2. So you understand what a program is doing if you read someone's code that does open a file for both reading and writing

Making `"files"` within your script

There are times in which your script will need `"external"` data. This data is typically stored in another file and read into your script through a filehandle. In some cases, however, this may not be the best way of handling it.

When someone copies your script, they may not realize that the external file needs to be copied as well. Another issue might be the permissions on the external file.

Instead of creating an external file, consider using the **__END__** token after your program code and place the data there:

```
#!perl
#files.pl
```

```
@names=<main::DATA>;
chomp (@names);
print "$names[0]\n";
__END__
Ted
Fred
Bob
Sue
```

Notes

- When you read from **<main::DATA>**, the data will be read from the **__END__** to the end of the file.

- Don't place any code after the **__END__** token!

- In many cases (such as the preceding example), it would be better to use a more "normal" method (such as @names=qw(Ted Fred Bob Sue) than using the **__END__** token. However, if there were 10,000 names to place in the array, then using this method would be a very good one!

Try it!

Change to the unit four "examples" directory and then execute the following command:

```
perl -d files.pl
```

Execute the following commands at the debugger prompt to practice using the embedded main::DATA filehandle:

```
print tell main::DATA;        #why is this not 0?  See note below.

$name=<main::DATA>;

print $name;

q
```

> **Important note**   Don't try to move around in the `main::DATA` `"file"`.
> Technically this includes the entire Perl script. Perl automatically moves the pointer
> to right after the __END__ token, so you can start reading from the data. But, if you
> seek back to the top, you are reading from the script itself (a handy thing to know
> if you ever want to review the code that is currently executing).

Locking files

On the surface, file locking is a simple concept. You want to make sure someone else
doesn't meddle with a file that you are writing data to. In reality, file locking is much
more complex.

To begin with, file locking isn't absolute (at least in UNIX and Linux); it's more of a
suggestion to the OS to lock the file. Processes that attempt write to files `"nicely"` will
adhere to this suggestion. However, processes don't have to be `"nice"`.

In addition, not every OS supports file locking. Since UNIX has long been a multiuser
environment, it does support file locking.

There are four types of file locking:

Symbolic Value	"Real" Value	Meaning
LOCK_SH	1	Shared lock (allows reading operations from other processes)
LOCK_EX	2	Exclusive lock (when you want to write to the file)
LOCK_NB	4	Non-blocking request
LOCK_UN	8	Unlock the file

Note about the symbolic values: Prior to version 5.004, the symbolic values didn't
exist. Using the `"Real"` values is safer.

Example of file locking

```perl
#!perl
#flock.pl

open (GROUP, ">>/tmp/group");
flock(GROUP, 2);
```

154

```perl
print GROUP "test::987:root";

close(GROUP);
```

The process of closing the filehandle also unlocks the file. You can have the file unlocked prior to closing the filehandle by using the following statement:

```perl
flock (GROUP, 8);
```

However, this often causes problems when the output of **print** statements hasn't been flushed (see the next section for more details regarding this).

Flushing output buffers

By default, the output of **print** statements doesn't go directly to the filehandle. Perl will store the output in a buffer until a newline character is printed:

```perl
#!/usr/bin/perl
#sleep1.pl

print "countdown!\n\n";
for ($i=10;$i>0;$i--) {
    print "$i \r";
    sleep 1;
}
print "Blast off!\n"
```

If the preceding example is run, "countdown!" will appear on the screen followed by what seems to be a pause of 10 seconds. After this pause, "Blast off!" will appear on the screen.

The "countdown numbers" don't appear since the output buffer isn't "flushed" until the newline character in the last **print** statement.

To solve this problem, flush the output buffer by changing the value of the **$|** variable:

```perl
#!perl
#sleep2.pl

print "countdown!\n\n";
$|=1;
```

```
for ($i=10;$i>0;$i--) {
   print "$i \r";
   sleep 1;
}
$|=0;
print "Blast off!\n"
```

Using select

The **select** statement discussed in a previous chapter also comes into play with the **$|** variable. The filehandle indicated by the last **select** statement is the one that is affected by this variable.

 Try it!

Change to the unit four "examples" directory and then execute the following commands:

perl sleep1.pl

perl sleep2.pl

Notice the difference in the output of these two commands. Determine why there is a difference based on the information provided in the previous section.

Additional resources

In each chapter, resources are provided to provide the learner with a source for more information. These resources may include downloadable source code or links to other books or articles that will provide you more information about the topic at hand.

Resources for this chapter can be found here:

https://github.com/Apress/pro-perl-programming

Lab exercises

Important notes

#1 If you did not finish the previous lab, either finish it before starting this lab or use the completed `parse3.pl`

provided in the lab answers folder.

#2 In this lab, you will be changing the `parse.txt` file. This is the file that has been used to provide the `data.pl`

---

script with the output data. In the event that you "`mess up`" this file, there is a "`backup copy`" called
`parse-orig.txt`. Just copy this over the "`messed up`" `parse.txt` file to return it to its original format.

Modify `parse3.pl` to include the following changes:

- Open the file `data.txt` for both reading and writing (make sure you lock the file).

- Read the data from the file into your array.

- When the script ends, write the data back into the file (don't forget to add newline characters back in if the user chooses option #1).

Save these changes into a file called `parse4.pl`.

Notes and hints

- Think about how your script will handle the file if it is "`new`" vs. if it has been modified.

When you have completed your work, compare your script against the `parse4.pl` file provided in lab answers.

CHAPTER 7

Pragmas

The intent behind pragmas is to modify the behavior of your Perl script. Pragmas are invoked with the **use** statement:

```
use strict;
```

To disable the use of a pragma, use the **no** statement:

```
no strict;
```

Note   Some pragmas cannot be turned off.

The purpose of this section is to review some of the useful pragmas. Some pragmas will not be discussed either because they are covered in another class or because they are beyond the scope of this class.

Pragma chart

The following chart lists some of the pragmas available in Perl. Note that different versions of Perl have different pragmas available. Many of these pragmas are covered in this chapter, but some are covered in other chapters of this book or are not covered in this book because they are specific to topics that are not related to the topics covered here.

Pragma	Meaning
autouse	Delays the operation of a **require** statement until one of the specified subroutines is called
constant	Defined constants during compile time
diagnostics	Issues verbose error messages

(continued)

W. "Bo" Rothwell, *Pro Perl Programming*, https://doi.org/10.1007/978-1-4842-5605-3_7

Pragma	Meaning
feature	Makes use of a new feature
lib	Modifies the @INC variable at compile time
locale	States to either use or ignore the current locale for built-in operations
overload	Overloads the basic Perl operations
strict	Prevents unwise statements
subs	Allows you to predeclare subroutines
vars	Allows you to predeclare global variables
warnings	Allows you to control warnings

The use strict pragma

There are three things you can tell Perl to be strict about: reference usage, subroutine usage, and variable usage:

use strict 'ref'

This will cause your program to exit if a symbolic reference is used. Symbolic references are a method of referring to variable and are not covered in this book.

use strict 'subs'

This feature will creates an error message for "barewords" (a bareword is an unquoted string that appears to be subroutine calls) that don't call a valid subroutine. For example, consider the following code:

```perl
#!perl
#subs.pl

use strict 'subs';
sub hello {
print "hello\n";
}
```

```
hello;     #Calls a valid subroutine, no problem
justatest; #Bareword that isn't a subroutine.
```

Try it!

Execute the following command:

`perl subs.pl`

Notice the error message that appears. Now, modify the subs.pl script by commenting out the "use strict", line and execute the command again:

`perl subs.pl`

Notice that no error message appears when the "justatest" subroutine is executed.

You may be wondering why when you run the subs.pl script without the **use strict 'subs'** pragma, no error occurs. It is fairly common that when you make a logical error in a Perl program, Perl tends to just ignore the problem completely. In this case, you attempted to call a function that doesn't exist, and Perl essentially said "ok, that isn't going to work, so I will just pretend like you didn't do that".

use strict 'vars'

This pragma will generate an error if a variable is used that

- Has not been declared as a **my** variable
- Isn't a fully qualified variable name
- Has not been declared as an **our** variable
- Has not been declared with a **use vars** statement

A fully qualified variable is one that includes its package namespace in the variable name. The following is just a brief introduction to using fully qualified variable names from the "main" namespace of your script.

While it is sometimes useful to have global variables, **use strict vars** doesn't allow this. If you want to use or modify variables from the "main" part (AKA "main" package) of your program, use the following syntax:

$main::var

The following program is an example of using global variables (Perl's default behavior):

```perl
#!perl
#usevars1.pl

use strict 'vars';

sub test {
    print "$total\n";
}

$total=100;
&test;
```

In this example, we are implementing **use strict vars**, which would cause compile errors if we didn't use fully qualified variable names:

perl usevars1.pl

Global symbol "$total" requires explicit package name (did you forget to declare "my $total"?) at usevars1.pl line 7.

Global symbol "$total" requires explicit package name (did you forget to declare "my $total"?) at usevars1.pl line 10.

Execution of usevars1.pl aborted due to compilation errors.

The following program shows a solution in which fully qualified variable names are used:

```perl
#!perl
#usevars2.pl

use strict 'vars';

sub test {
    print "$main::total\n";
}
```

```
$main::total=100;
&test;
```

If you are asking yourself "why not declare the $total variable as a my variable", keep in mind that a **my** variable would only exist in the main part of the program. Because **my** variables are scoped, the subroutine would not have access to the $total variable. In most cases this is good practice, but there are use cases in which being able to share a variable between the main program and a subroutine (or between different subroutines) is advantageous.

Notes regarding **use strict**

- The statement **use strict** will enforce all restrictions (refs, subs, and vars).

- Perl built-in variables are not affected by **use strict vars**.

- The concept of **our** variables and **use vars** variables is covered later in this chapter.

Predeclaring subroutines

Typically, you need to create a subroutine prior to using it. For example, the following code won't produce any output since the subroutine isn't declared until after it is called:

```
#!perl
#sub1.pl

hello;

sub hello {
    print "hi there\n";
}
```

This can cause problems, especially if you are using **use strict subs**. This is because when the subroutine call is made, the subroutine hasn't officially been declared yet. This is a very subtle, yet important, feature of Perl. While all of the Perl code is compiled before it is executed (hence syntax errors result in compile time failures), some actions are run time operations.

For example, in the following program, the hello subroutine is compiled (in other words, created) during compile time, but it doesn't officially exist for Perl until its definition appears in the Perl program:

```perl
#!perl
#sub2.pl

use strict subs;

hello;

sub hello {
   print "hi there\n";
}
```

Using **use subs** you can "predefine" subroutines. The process of "predefining" the subroutine essentially says from this moment on, I declare this a valid subroutine. See the following for an example:

```perl
#!perl
#sub3.pl

use subs qw(hello);
use strict subs;

hello;

sub hello {
   print "hi there\n";
}
```

Notes

- Once invoked, you cannot use **no subs** to undo a **use subs** statement.

- If you use the ampersand character before the function name, you do not have to predeclare subroutines that are placed after they are called.

- The **use subs qw(hello)** statement is the same as invoking **sub hello {}**.

164

Try it!

Execute the following command:

```
perl sub1.pl
```

Notice that no output that appears. The subroutine isn't executed, and no error occurs either. Now, execute the following command:

```
perl sub2.pl
```

Notice that an error message appears when the "hello" subroutine is executed. This is because even though the subroutine was created at compile time, it hasn't been declared during run time. Now, execute the following command:

```
perl sub3.pl
```

The "use subs" statement declares the "hello" subroutine to be the one that was created at compile time; no error occurs, and the "hello" subroutine executes normally.

Before moving forward, it is important to answer the question: Why should I put the subroutine at the bottom of the program rather than the top? Frankly, the reason for this is essentially "because I can and because it is easier to find the start of the main part of the program".

To understand this, consider the following scenario: You have a Perl program of about 10,000 lines of code with about 30 subroutines. Typically, those subroutines would be placed at the top of the program and the main program placed toward the bottom of the script. If someone were to read your code, they would need to search through the file to find the main part of the program and start reading there. Putting the main part of the program at the top makes is a bit more readable.

Having the main part of the program at the top of the code to make the program more readable might not be a good enough reason for you to use this technique, especially when you consider there is a fairly significant issue that results from this technique. To understand this issue, consider the following code:

```
#!perl
#sub4.pl
```

```
sub hello {
    print "hi there, $name\n";
}

my $name="Ted";
hello;
```

The outcome of sub4.pl:

```
perl sub4.pl
hi there,
```

As expected, the hello subroutine can't access the contents of the $name variable because it is a my variable that was created in the main package. Now consider the following program in which the subroutine is declared after the main part of the program:

```
#!perl
#sub5.pl
use subs qw(hello);

my $name="Ted";
hello;

sub hello {
    print "hi there, $name\n";
}
```

The outcome of sub5.pl:

```
perl sub5.pl
hi there, Ted
```

How is this possible? The scope of a variable exists from the point it is declared until the end of the closure of the area in which the variable is declared. This is inclusive of other blocks of code. You probably already realize this because you have very likely written code like the following fragment:

```
my $result=100;
while (some condition here) {
    print $result;   #this is the my variable from above
}
```

You expect the **my** variable **$result** to be available within the **while** loop, but consider that the **while** loop has its own scope that allows you to create a **my** variable that only would exist within the loop:

```perl
my $result=100;
while (some condition here) {
    my $test=99;
    print $result; #this is the my variable from above
}
print $result;  #still the original my variable
print $test;    #not declared as this only exists in the while loop
```

In other words, if you put the subroutines as the bottom part of your program, every subroutine will have access to every my variable in the main part of your program. There is, however, a solution to this problem: create another level of scope as shown in the following example.

```perl
#!perl
#sub6.pl

use subs qw(hello);

{
my $name="Ted";
hello;
}

sub hello {
    print "hi there, $name\n";
}
```

The outcome of sub6.pl:

```perl
perl sub6.pl
hi there,
```

Predeclaring global variables

When you refer to an undeclared variable, Perl either returns a 0 or a null string:

```
#!perl
#var1.pl

print "The total is $total\n";
print "The result is ", $total+5, "\n";
```

This is a somewhat commonly used feature in Perl. In fact, it could be used to test if a variable has been defined (although the defined function is better than the following technique which would also print "no" if $test was set to 0 or ""):

```
  DB<1> if ($test) {print "yes";} else {print "no";}
no
  DB<2> $test="abc"

  DB<3> if ($test) {print "yes";} else {print "no";}
yes
```

In small Perl scripts, using an undeclared variable can often be convenient. However, if you invoke "**use strict vars**", you will receive an error message as in the following program:

```
#!perl
#var2.pl

use strict vars;

print "The total is $total\n";
print "The result is ", $total+5, "\n";
```

To be able to use a variable prior to having it set, you can use the statement **use vars**. This is essentially saying "ok, I haven't set this variable yet, but for the sake of the **use strict** pragma, pretend this is a valid variable". Here is an example:

```
#!perl
#var3.pl

use strict vars;
use vars qw($total);
```

```
print "The total is $total\n";
print "The result is ", $total+5, "\n";
```

This is very useful when you are not sure if a variable is set or not. When you use **strict vars**, even a **defined** statement will fail:

```
#!perl
#var4.pl

use strict vars;

if (defined ($total))                    #This will result in an error
   {print "hey, it's here!\n";}
else
   {print "It's not there!\n";}
```

When you use **use vars**, the **defined** statement will not fail:

```
#!perl
#var5.pl

use strict vars;
use vars qw($total);

if (defined ($total))
   {print "hey, it's here!\n";}
else
   {print "It's not there!\n";}
```

Notes

- Once invoked, you cannot use **no vars** to undo a **use vars** statement.

- Note that the variable that is declared by a **use vars** statement is not a my variable. It belongs to the package it was declared in (in the previous example, the "main" package).

- If you switch packages, then the use vars statement no longer applies, and an error will occur. This will be demonstrated later in this section.

use vars is obsolete

As of Perl 5.6, **use vars** is considered to be obsolete. It is covered in this book for the following reasons:

1. You may wish to write code that is backward compatible to older versions of Perl. If so, you may want to continue to use the **use vars** statement.

2. While **use vars** is considered to be obsolete, it still performs the same function that is always has. As a result, you will still see it being used in another programmer's code.

3. Part of being a Perl programmer is maintaining legacy code. There are still many older Perl scripts that use the use vars pragma.

Instead of using **use vars**, you should use the **our** statement to "globally declare" a variable. Much like **use vars**, specifying the **our** statement will allow you to use a variable without its fully qualified name while your code has **use strict** implemented:

```perl
#!perl
#var6.pl

use strict vars;
our $total;

if (defined ($total))
   {print "hey, it's here!\n";}
else
   {print "It's not there!\n";}
```

The **our** statement often creates a lot of confusion among Perl programmers (especially novice Perl programmers). According to the Perl man pages, the **our** statement '...has the same scoping rules as a "my" declaration, but does not create a local variable'. In a sense, an "our" variable is somewhat of a merge between a **my** variable and a variable declared with the **use vars** statement.

Remember that the **use vars** statement allowed you to specify $var instead of **$PackageName::var** (*PackageName* is the name of the package the variable was declared in), and this pertained to the package itself. A "my" variable falls completely outside the realm of packages; it exists only in its own "area".

An "our" variable allows you to specify $var instead of **$PackageName::var**. So, like variables created with **use vars**, the variable exists inside a package. However, if you enter a new package, the "our" variable can still be accessed by specifying $var (you don't need to specify **$PackageName::var**). If your leaves the scope area that the **our** variable was created in, you need to use the fully qualified name (**$PackageName::var**) to access the variable again. This means that unlike **my** variables which are destroyed once the program leaves the scope that the variable was declared in, **our** variables still exist.

All three variable types ("use vars", "my", and "our") are allowed when "use strict 'vars'" is in force. The following example displays the differences between the three variable types:

```perl
#!perl
#our.pl

{package ABC;  #Beginning of scope and ABC package

our($our_var)="xyz";                #part of ABC package
my($my_var)="123";                  #part of scope only
use vars qw($use_var);              #declares $$ABC::use_var
$use_var="abc";                     #part of ABC package

print "\$our_var = $our_var\n";
print "\$my_var = $my_var\n";
print "\$use_var = $use_var\n";

package New;
print "\$our_var = $our_var\n";     #Displays $ABC::our_var
print "\$my_var = $my_var\n";       #Displays "scoped" $my_var
print "\$use_var = $use_var\n";     #Doesn't exist - wrong package

}                                   #End of Scope

print "\$our_var = $our_var\n";     #Doesn't exist - out of scope & wrong
                                    package
print "\$my_var = $my_var\n";       #Doesn't exist - out of scope
print "\$use_var = $use_var\n";     #Doesn't exist - wrong package
```

171

Output of our.pl:

our.pl

```
$our_var = xyz
$my_var = 123
$use_var = abc
$our_var = xyz
$my_var = 123
$use_var =
$our_var =
$my_var =
$use_var =
```

Try it!

Execute the following command:

`perl var2.pl`

Notice the error that occurs due to the "use strict" statement. Now, execute the following command:

`perl var3.pl`

Notice that no error occurs. The variable now has a "global-like" quality to it. Now, execute the following command:

`perl var6.pl`

Again, no error occurs. The "use var" pragma is very similar to the "our" statement. In both cases you can use the variable without using a fully qualified name.

Bonus: Add the **use strict** statement to the **our.pl** program and then execute it. Notice that an error will occur. Comment out the line that the error occurs on, and run the program again. Another (different) error will occur. Continue to comment out each error, and run the program until no errors occur.

Using new features

Starting in Perl 5.10, new features are included via the **use feature** pragma. To make use of a new feature, you use the following syntax:

`use feature "feature_name";`

Some of the new features are taken from Perl 6. Other features may provide backward compatibility to older versions of Perl 5 or may provide new functionality to Perl 5. Note that some of these features are "experimental", which means they may be discontinued in future releases. Use such features sparingly.

These new features in Perl 5.10 include

- **say** – A replacement for print that automatically prints a newline character.

- **state** – A replacement for my that differs in that it will retain previously set values

- **switch** – Provides a "switch" statement (although the statement is actually called **given**, not switch)

As new versions of Perl are introduced, new features are also added. For example, the following is a partial list of features that have been introduced in different releases of Perl:

- **current_sub** – Allows you to determine the current subroutine by returning a reference to the subroutine when you use the __SUB__ token. Introduced in Perl 5.16

- **array_base** – Allows the use of the $[variable, a variable that is used in conjunction with arrays. Introduced in Perl 5.16

Note   Not all of the available features are covered in this book as some are designed for very specific use cases. The purpose of this section is to expose you to the functionality and purpose of the **feature** pragma, not to cover all of the new features. Consult the **use feature** documentation for additional features.

Example of use feature 'say' and use feature 'state'

Perhaps the most useful of the new features, or at least the most commonly used, are the **state** and **say** features. With the **state** feature, Perl now has stateful variables – variables whose values are persistent from one subroutine call to another. The **say** feature is really designed to provide a more programmer-friendly **print** statement (no longer do you have to end your **print** string with a newline character):

```perl
#!perl
#feature-1.pl

use feature 'state';
use feature 'say';

sub show {
    state $var;
    say "The variable is set to $var";
    $var=100;
}

&show;
&show;
```

Example of use feature "switch"

It is slightly confusing that asking for the "switch" feature gives you access to a function called "given"; however, the **given** function acts like a **switch** statement:

```perl
#!perl
#given.pl

use feature "switch";   #Provides access to the given statement

print "Please enter 'yes' or 'no': ";
$response=<STDIN>;
chomp $response;
```

```
given ($response) {
        when ("yes") {print "You agree!\n"; }
        when ("no")  {print "Bummer, you don't agree\n"; }
        default     {print "Maybe next time\n"; }
}
```

Note   Depending on the version of Perl that you are using, you may receive the following messages:

given is experimental at `given.pl` line 10.

when is experimental at `given.pl` line 11.

when is experimental at `given.pl` line 12.

This is normal output as these features may change in the future.

Using all features of a specific Perl version

Both the `'say'` and `'state'` features are available in Perl 5.10. To load both features (and all others available in this version), use the following code:

```
#!perl
#feature-2.pl

use 5.010;

sub show {
   state $var;
   say "The variable is set to $var";
   $var=100;
}
&show;
&show;
```

Try it!

Execute the following command to enter the Perl debugger:

```
perl -d -e "1;"
```

Execute the following code in the debugger:

```
print "hello"; print "goodbye";
```

Notice that there is no "newline" character between the outputs of the two "print" statements. Now execute the following commands:

```
use feature "say";
```

```
say "hello"; say "goodbye";
```

Notice that the newline character is automatically added to the output of each "say" statement. Recall that this feature, along with "state" and "switch", was added in Perl 5.10. Visit the Perl documentation (http://perldoc.perl.org), select the version of Perl that you are using from the "Perl Version" drop-down list, and then review the documentation of the "feature" pragma to see what other features are available for the version of Perl that you are using.

Using locale

Some Perl statements can behave differently based on the locale. For example, the numeric fields of format statements assume that the decimal point character is a period (.), while in some locales, a comma (,) is used.

To tell Perl to make use of a different locale, the **locale** pragma can be used. Locale settings include date/time, currency, numeric, and other formats. Perl will query the operating system for the current locale, which can be configured either system-wide or for individual users on most operating systems.

You can either use the locale settings throughout your entire program by stating **use locale** at the top of your program or use the locale settings in a block:

```
#not using locale settings here
{
use locale;  #using locale settings here
}
#not using locale settings here
```

Final note about pragmas

This chapter was designed to introduce you to the concept of pragmas as well as cover many of the commonly used Perl pragmas. There are certainly more pragmas, some of which are covered in different parts of this book (the re pragmas, e.g., was introduced in Chapter 2).

Not all pragmas are covered in this book for a couple of reasons:

1. Some pragmas are either esoteric or pertain to very specific Perl features that are not covered in this book.

2. Some pragmas are only available for specific versions of Perl. Using these sorts of pragmas can lead to backward dependency issues (and, in cases of experimental pragmas, forward dependency issues).

To learn more about other pragmas, review the `"pragmas"` documentation at `http://perldoc.perl.org`.

Additional resources

In each chapter, resources are provided to provide the learner with a source for more information. These resources may include downloadable source code or links to other books or articles that will provide you more information about the topic at hand.

Resources for this chapter can be found here:

`https://github.com/Apress/pro-perl-programming`

Lab exercises

Important note   If you did not finish the previous lab, either finish it before starting this lab or use the completed `parse4.pl` provided in the lab answers folder.

Modify `parse4.pl` to include the following changes:

- Implement "`use strict`". Note that unless you have been using scoped variables or fully qualified variable names, you are likely to see a lot of errors after implementing this pragma. Choose which variable should be scoped, fully qualified, or "`global-like`" ("`use vars`" or "`our`" variables), and make the necessary changes to your program.

- Move your subroutines to the bottom of your script.

Save these changes into a file called `parse5.pl`.

When you have completed your work, compare your script against the `parse5.pl` file provided in lab answers.

CHAPTER 8

Exploring Useful Built-in Modules

Years ago, while assisting a client with a Perl program, the client demonstrated a function that he was very proud of. The purpose of this function was to overcome the limitations of Perl and allow for larger floating point numbers. The code itself was a few hundred lines long, took weeks of work, and was still a bit buggy.

In one of those `"good news, bad news"` situations, I introduced the client to the Math::BigFloat module, a module that would have solved the client's problem in minutes, not weeks, providing a solution that didn't contain the bugs and idiosyncrasies of the client's code. The client was grateful but also unhappy with the wasted time and effort spent on his own code.

There are hundreds of built-in Perl modules (and thousands more available on `www.cpan.org/`). Some of these modules are often used, while some are a bit more rare. The purpose of this chapter is to introduce you to some of the more commonly used built-in modules and to get you to think `"let me see if that already exists"` before you start writing any code.

Built-in modules

Perl modules (sometime called libraries) are files that contain reusable code. These libraries can either be created by you, built-in to Perl, or downloaded from the Internet.

179

© William "Bo" Rothwell of One Course Source, Inc. 2020
W. "Bo" Rothwell, *Pro Perl Programming*, https://doi.org/10.1007/978-1-4842-5605-3_8

This unit focuses on using useful built-in modules. These modules are located in directories indicated by the elements in the **@INC** variable. The contents of this variable can vary depending on the platform you run Perl on and the version or distribution of Perl. For example, the following was executed on a Windows system with Strawberry Perl installed:

```
DB<1> print "@INC"
C:/Strawberry/perl/site/lib C:/Strawberry/perl/vendor/lib C:/Strawberry/
perl/lib
```

Note   For detailed documentation of Perl modules, go to **perldoc.perl.org** or **cpan.org**.

Manipulate **@INC** at compile time

If you install your own modules, you may not be able to put them in one of the default locations (see output above). Typically, only the system administrator can modify these directories.

In such cases, you will want to modify the **@INC** variable during compile time. To do this, use the **lib** pragma:

```
#!perl
#6_lib.pl

use lib "perl_class";

print "@INC", "\n";
```

The argument to the **use lib** statement will be pre-appended to the **@INC** variable. Note that you can't simply modify the @INC using normal array manipulation method because those are executed at run time, while modules are loaded at compile time.

There is, however, an alternative method. The use lib isn't very flexible in that it always pre-appends to the @INC variable. Perhaps you would rather the new directory be appended to the @INC variable. This could be done with a BEGIN block:

```
BEGIN {

push (@INC, "perl_class);
}
```

Code in a BEGIN block is executed during compile time.

Determining the location of loaded modules

Once a module has been loaded, the original location of the module is stored in the %INC associative array:

```
#!perl
#6_inc.pl

use Cwd;

foreach $key (keys %INC) {
   print "$key ->> $INC{$key}\n";
}
```

Output of the preceding program on a Linux system:

```
[student@linux1 student]$ perl 6_inc.pl
Carp.pm ->> /usr/local/lib/perl5/5.02801/Carp.pm
Cwd.pm ->> /usr/local/lib/perl5/5.02801/Cwd.pm
Exporter.pm ->> /usr/local/lib/perl5/5.02801/Exporter.pm
```

Try it!

Execute the following command to start the Perl debugger:

```
perl -d -e "1;"
```

Execute the following command in the debugger to display the location of the module search path:

```
print "@INC";
```

Execute the following command in the debugger to load a module and determine its location:

```
use File::Copy;

print $INC{"File/Copy.pm"};
```

Loading modules as needed

Modules can be loaded during run time only as needed by using the **use autouse** pragma. The syntax for this is

use autouse 'Cwd' => qw(cwd);

If the **cwd** function is never used in the program, then the **Cwd** module is never loaded. The advantage of this technique is that your program might execute faster. More technically, the compile process would be faster, and, if they module is never needed, the entire compile + execution time would be faster. However, if the module is needed at some point in the program, it would be loaded during execution time.

This may pose problems. Module loading is normally a compile time operation as certain checks (like the most basic "is the module available" check) are best performed during compile time. Most of the time you would want these checks to be done at compile time, not in the middle of the execution of the program where they might cause the program to crash.

So, should you use the **autouse** pragma? It is mostly a judgment call, but if you are loading built-in modules, which should certainly be available and shouldn't cause any load time errors, then the **autouse** pragma is fairly safe. However, if you always (or almost always) use code from the module, it is best to load it during compile time with a regular **use** statement. Only consider using the **autouse** pragma when the use of the code of a module is based on some sort of condition of your code.

Consult the WARNING section of the **autouse** pragma documentation for more details.

Module table

There are many modules available with the default installation of Perl. Keep in mind that there are hundreds of modules and some of the most common used modules are described in the following table:

Module or group	Meaning
AutoSplit	Split a package for autoloading
Benchmark	Used to benchmark the running time of code
CPAN	Setup and interface to the Comprehensive Perl Archive Network
Carp	Used for debugging; gives warning messages
Class	Allows for "struct-like" data structures
Cwd	Internal method of displaying current directory
Data	Used to display data in different formats
English	Allows you to use less cryptic variable names
Env	Imports environment variables
Exporter	Used in modules to specify default import methods
Fatal	Change the outcome of failed statements with die
File	A group of modules that deals with files
GDBM_File	Gives access to gdbm lib
Getopts	Used to handle command line arguments
Math	A group of modules that deal with math
Sys	A group of modules that gains access to system information
Text	A group of modules that manipulate text

Cwd

The Cwd module provides some functions for displaying the current working directory and changing your current directory:

Function	Purpose
cwd	A portable method of getting the current working directory
getcwd	Displays current working directory
fastcwd	A faster running of getcwd

cwd

The **cwd** statement is normally the best method to use to display your current working directory. It uses the OS architecture to determine the current working directory. An example of **cwd** on a Linux system:

```
DB<1> use Cwd
DB<2> print cwd
/etc/skel
```

Windows example of cwd:

```
DB<1> use Cwd
DB<2> print cwd
C:/Windows
```

getcwd

Displays current working directory but may not be portable. Avoid if you are trying to create a portable script. An example of **getcwd** on a Linux system:

```
DB<1> use Cwd
DB<2> print getcwd
/etc/skel
```

fastcwd

The **fastcwd** statement is a faster (and less safe) method of **getcwd**. As the Perl man pages state "`...it might conceivably chdir() you out of a directory that it can't chdir() you back into`". The **chdir()** function is used to change from one directory to another. An example of **fastcwd** on a Linux system:

```
DB<1> use Cwd
DB<2> print fastcwd
/etc/skel
```

Why not use a system statement?

Many operating systems provide command that returns the current directory. While you could determine the current directory by using an OS command with a **system** statement, there are some drawbacks. The following is an example on a Linux system:

```
DB<1> system "pwd"
/etc/skel
DB<2> chdir("/etc")
DB<3> system "pwd"
/etc
```

The disadvantages of using this method:

- It's often slower than built-in modules because a separate operating system shell needs to be spawned.

- It makes your script less portable (the above will only work for UNIX- and Linux-based systems).

- It makes your script more user-dependent (e.g., the user might have an alias for "`pwd`").

A good rule of thumb: If you can do it within Perl, then do it within Perl!

Env

Environment variables are variables provided by the operating system or the system's shell. These variables often contain very useful information, such as the username of the person running the program. By default, Perl stores environment variables in a hash. The Env module will allow you to import these variables into scalar variables that often are easier to work with than hashes:

```
DB<1> print $ENV{HOME}
/export/home/student2
DB<2> print $HOME

DB<3> use Env
DB<4> print $HOME
/export/home/student2
```

Try it!

Execute the following command to start the Perl debugger:

```
perl -d -e "1;"
```

Environment variables are different depending on your operating system. For example, on Linux systems, $ENV{HOME} contains the current user's home directory path. On Windows this information is in two %ENV keys: HOMEDRIVE and HOMEPATH. Execute the following code which should allow you to view the current's user's home directory path in either Linux or Windows (the \ is required before pressing the <ENTER> key to allow for multiline statements in the Perl debugger):

```
use Env;
if ($HOME)                              \
{                                       \
    print "$HOME\n";                    \
}                                       \
```

```
else                            \
{                               \
   print "$HOMEDRIVE$HOMEPATH\n";   \
}
```

> **Note** Environment variables are very useful, but you should remember that they are specific to the platform. In other words, the environment variables provided by Windows is different than the environment variables provided by Linux. If your program is not designed to be portable, using environment variables should not pose a problem.

File modules

There are many modules in the File group. This section covers some of the most useful of these modules.

File::Basename

This module will split up a pathname using the OS's default delimiter for filenames. The OS type is determined by looking at the **$^O** variable. An example:

```
DB<1> #This is on a UNIX machine
DB<2> print "$^O"
solaris
DB<3> use File::Basename
DB<4> ($base, $path) = fileparse("/usr/local/bin/test.txt")
DB<5> print $base
test.txt
DB<6> print $path
/usr/local/bin/
```

File::Compare

This module will check to see if two files are the same or not. It returns 0 if the two files are equal, 1 if they are unequal, or -1 if an error occurred.

```
DB<1> use File::Compare
DB<2> print compare ("/etc/group", "/tmp/group")
0
DB<3> print compare ("/etc/passwd", "/etc/group")
1
DB<4> print compare ("/etc/passwd", "/etc/shadow")
1
DB<5> print compare ("/etc/passwd", "/etc/junk")
-1
```

File::Compare can handle binary files as well as text files:

```
DB<1> print compare ("/usr/bin/ls", "/usr/ucb/ls")
1
```

File::Copy

While there is a built-in Perl **rename** statement, there isn't any built-in copy statement. With the File::Copy module, you can copy files:

```
DB<1> use File::Copy
DB<2> copy ("/etc/group", "/tmp/group")
```

File::Path

Two of Perl's built-in statements, **mkdir** and **rmdir**, are extremely limited. The **mkdir** statement is limited because the path up until the new directory must currently exist. The following will fail because the "data" directory doesn't exist:

```
DB<1> mkdir ("/tmp/data/newlogs", 0755) || warn "could not make dir"
could not make dir at (eval 4) line 2, <IN> chunk 1.
```

The **rmdir** statement is limited because it will only delete empty directories. The solution to both of these problems is the File::Path module. This module provides two new statements: **mkpath** and **rmtree**.

The **mkpath** statement will make a directory and its parent directories if needed. It takes three arguments:

1) The name of the path to create

2) A value to indicate if the command should print the name of each directory that is created (1=yes, 0=no)

3) The permissions of the new directories (defaults to 0777)

An example of **mkpath**:

```
DB<1> use File::Path
DB<2> mkpath ("/tmp/data/newlogs", 1, 0755)
mkdir /tmp/data
mkdir /tmp/data/newlogs
```

The **rmtree** statement will remove a directory tree (much like the UNIX command "rm -r"). This statement also takes three arguments:

1) The name of the directory structure to delete

2) A value to indicate if the command should print the name of each file and directory and the action that is being taken (1=yes, 0=no)

3) A value to indicate if **rmtree** should skip files that you cannot delete (1=yes, 0=no)

An example of **rmtree**:

```
DB<1> use File::Path
DB<2> rmtree ("/tmp/skel", 1, 1)
unlink /tmp/skel/local.login
unlink /tmp/skel/local.profile
unlink /tmp/skel/.profile
unlink /tmp/skel/local.cshrc
rmdir /tmp/skel
```

File::Find

The File::Find module provides two subroutines that will allow you to traverse a directory tree and perform actions: **find** and **finddepth**. The basic syntax is

find (\&wanted, @directorys_to_search);

The \&wanted is a subroutine reference to wanted. References are discussed in detail in a later class. The subroutine does not have to be called wanted().

This **wanted** function accepts no arguments but creates three variables for use within the function:

- $File::Find::dir stores the current directory name.

- $_ stores the current filename within that directory.

- $File::Find::name stores the complete pathname to the file.

See the following for an example of this module:

```perl
#!perl
#6_find-1.pl

use File::Find;

sub display {
    print "$_\n";
}

find (\&display, "..");
```

The **wanted** function has other features; consult the documentation for this module (http://perldoc.perl.org/File/Find.html#The-wanted-function).

Try it!

Switch to the "unit6" examples directory and then execute the following command:

```
perl 6_find-1.pl
```

This should list all of the files from the "examples" directory down. To make this more useful, replace the print line in this file with the following:

```
if (/^6/) {
    print "$_\n";
}
```

This should only print the files that begin with the number 6. This demonstrates that the find command will find ALL files; it is really up to you to create a filtering function.

Additional useful file modules

There are some additional file modules that you should consider exploring:

- **File::DosGlob** – Provides DOS-based wildcard behavior for filename matching.

- **File::Fetch** – A very useful module which allows you to "fetch" a file from a remote location (or even a local location) using ftp, http, file, git, or rsync.

- **File::Spec** – Provides a host of useful utilities that allow you to perform platform-specific operations on the filesystem. For example, the **devnull** function returns a string of the null device for the current platform. There are about 20 functions in all, many of which provide common filesystem operations that you would otherwise need to create code for or rely on **system** statements.

- **File::Spec::** *platform* – This doesn't represent a single module but rather a collection of modules. Replace **platform** with Mac, OS2, Unix, Win32, or others for access to functions specific to that platform.

Math modules

There are many modules in the Math group. This section covers some of the most useful of these modules.

Math::BigFloat

Normally, the precision of floating point numbers is dependent on the OS's limits. While you can create a scalar variable that "appears" to be a big floating-point number, as soon as it is used as a number, Perl will round it off to fit the system's limit:

```
DB<1> $num="1.45645645645645645645645645645645645456456"
DB<2> print $num+1
2.45645645645646
```

To overcome this limit, use the Math::BigFloat module:

```
DB<1> use Math::BigFloat
DB<2> $num2 = new Math::BigFloat "1.45645645645645645645645645645645645456456"
DB<3> print $num2+1
2.45645645645645645645645645645645645456456
```

Math::Trig

With this function, you can perform trigonometric functions:

```
DB<1> use Math::Trig
DB<2> print tan(0.8)
1.02963855705036
DB<3> print pi/4
0.785398163397448
DB<4> print sin(.7)
0.644217687237691
```

For a complete listing of all of the trig functions, look at the man page for Math::Trig.

Additional useful math modules

There are some additional File modules that you should consider exploring:

- **Math::BigInt** – Like Math::BigFloat but only for integers.

- **Math::BigRat** – Like Math::BigFloat but only for rational numbers.

- **Math::Complex** – Provides mathematical operations for complex numbers.

Sys modules

One of the modules in the Sys group of modules is **Sys::Hostname**. This module will attempt (using several methods) to return the system's host name:

```
DB<1> use Sys::Hostname
DB<2> $hostname=hostname
DB<3> print $hostname
rainbow
```

The methods used are system dependent, so it will often work on different platforms.

Another potentially useful Sys module is **Sys::Syslog**. This provides an interface to the syslog service. This allows you to send log file entries to the system logger, which in turn sends this data to actual log files or other locations (remote log servers, user terminals, etc.).

The **Sys::Syslog** module is limited in that it is designed to work on Unix systems (and, to some extent, Linux systems), and it doesn't work with some services, like journald.

Text

The Text group of modules contains subroutines that modify text. This section covers some of the most useful of these modules.

Text::Tabs

This module contains two subroutines:

expand – Expands tabs just like the UNIX command expand

unexpand – Compresses spaces into tabs just like the UNIX command unexpand

To use the **expand** statement, first set a variable called **$tabstop** to indicate where the tab stops should be. Then, just use the **expand** statement:

```
DB<1> use Text::Tabs
DB<2> $tabstop=3
DB<3> @line=("A tab:    Two more            the end")
DB<4> @line=expand(@line)
DB<5> print $line[0]
A tab:    Two more      the end
```

The **unexpand** statement will replace spaces with tabs:

```
DB<1> use Text::Tabs
DB<2> $tabstop=5
DB<3> @line=("Here are ten spaces:             Here is five:     Finished!")
DB<4> @line=unexpand(@line)
DB<5> print $line[0]
Here are ten spaces:                 Here is five:        Finished!
```

Text::Wrap

The purpose of the Text::Wrap module is to be able to break up a paragraph "nicely" across multiple lines. The **wrap** statement will format a paragraph by breaking up lines on word boundaries. You can also "indent" text with spaces or tabs.

The format of the **wrap** statement:

```
wrap (first_line_indent, additional_line_indent, string_to_format)
```

In the following example, **wrap** will break the string on word boundaries and place a tab before the first line:

```perl
#!perl
#wrap1.pl

use Text::Wrap qw(wrap $columns);

$line="This is an example of how you can break up text into formatted
paragraphs.  This process is done by professionals on a closed track. Don't
attempt this at home!";

print "$line\n\n\n";

$columns=40;
print wrap ("\t", "", $line);
```

In this example, **wrap** will break the string on word boundaries and place a tab before all lines:

```perl
#!perl
#wrap2.pl

use Text::Wrap qw(wrap $columns);

$line="This is an example of how you can break up text into formatted
paragraphs.  This process is done by professionals on a closed track. Don't
attempt this at home!";

print "$line\n\n\n";

$columns=40;
print wrap ("\t", "\t", $line);
```

Try it!

Switch to the "unit6" examples directory and then execute the following command:

```
perl wrap1.pl
```

Notice that only the first line of the output is indented. Now execute the following command, and notice that all lines are indented:

```
perl wrap1.pl
```

Review the code for these two scripts, and determine why there is a difference in the output.

Fatal

Many Perl statements return `"true"` if they succeed or `"false"` if they fail. The Fatal module can be used to modify the behavior of such statements.

Instead of having these statements just return a value, Fatal can be used to have your script **die** if the statement fails. The syntax of Fatal:

use Fatal qw(commands_to_affect);

In the following example, if the **open** statement fails, the script will **die**:

```
#!perl
#fatal.pl

use Fatal qw (open);

open (GROUP, "</tmp/junkfile");

print "see...the program stopped!";
```

Benchmark

The Benchmark module helps you perform benchmarking tasks on your code. It provides many features that you can make use of, including

- **new** – Returns the current time
- **timediff** – Returns the difference between two times
- **timestr** – Converts times into `"understandable"` formats
- **timeit** – Runs a chunk of code once

- **timethis** – Runs a chunk of code several times

- **timethese** – Runs several chunks of code several times

Note that Benchmark is an OO-based module. This may result in some unusual looking code (unless you understand OO Perl).

See the following for an example:

```perl
#!perl
#benchmark-1.pl

use Benchmark;

$|=1; print "wait";
$t0 = Benchmark->new;

for (1..10) {
   print ".";
   sleep 1;
}

$t1 = Benchmark->new;

$td = timediff($t1, $t0);
print "the code took:",timestr($td),"\n";
```

See the Benchmark documentation for more details (http://perldoc.perl.org/ Benchmark.html).

Getopt::Std

The **Getopt::Std** module is standard in Perl. It provides you with an easy way to parse command-line arguments that are passed in by users. Consider the following code:

```perl
#!perl
#std_opt1.pl

use Getopt::Std;

getopts('a:b:c:');
```

```perl
print "$opt_a\n";
print "$opt_b\n";
print "$opt_c\n";
```

In the previous example, the **getopts** function defined three valid options: -a, -b, and -c. If these options are used, then the argument passed to the options are assigned to $opt_a, $opt_b, or $opt_c:

```
ocs% perl std_opt1.pl -a "test" -c "null"
test

null
```

The arguments that are parsed are also stripped off of the @ARGV array:

```perl
#!perl
#std_opt2.pl

use Getopt::Std;

getopts('a:b:c:');

print "$opt_a\n";
print "$opt_b\n";
print "$opt_c\n";
print "@ARGV\n"   #prints nothing, @ARGV now empty

ocs% perl std_opt2.pl -a "test" -c "null"
test

null
```

You can also have the option/arguments placed into a hash:

```perl
#!perl
#std_opt3.pl

use Getopt::Std;

getopts('a:b:c:', \%ops);
```

```perl
print "$ops{a}\n";
print "$ops{b}\n";
print "$ops{c}\n";
```

If you want some options to have arguments and others to be simple booleans, place a ":" character after the options that are to have arguments (the rest will be booleans):

```perl
#!perl
#std_opt4.pl

use Getopt::Std;

getopts('abc:');

print "$opt_a\n";
print "$opt_b\n";
print "$opt_c\n";
```

To tell the **getops** function to stop looking at arguments, use a -- option (-- will be removed from the @ARGV array):

```
ocs% perl std_opt4.pl -a -b -- -c "null"
```

If an unknown argument is passed, the **getopts** function will return false, and the program will end via a **die** statement:

```perl
#!perl
#std_opt5.pl

use Getopt::Std;

getopts('abc:') || die;

print "$opt_a\n";
print "$opt_b\n";
print "$opt_c\n";
print "@ARGV\n"
```

```
ocs% perl std_opt5.pl -a -b -d
Unknown option: d
Died at std_opt5.pl line 6.
```

Getopt::Long

The **Getopt::Long** module is standard in Perl. It provides you with more advanced techniques to parsing command-line options than **Getopt::Std**.

Instead of using simple arguments like -a, -b, and -c, with **Getopt::Long**, you use options like --all, --verbose, and --catchall. These options will be easier to remember and will "self-document". Simple example:

```perl
#!perl
#long_opt1.pl

use Getopt::Long;

GetOptions ('verbose' => \$verbose, 'all' => \$all, "catchall" => \$catch);

print "$verbose\n";
print "$all\n";
print "$catch\n";
print "@ARGV\n"
```

One nice feature of the **GetOptions** function is the ability to specify the "opposite" of an option. For example, the following will allow for both a "--verbose" and a "--noverbose" option:

```perl
#!perl
#long_opt2.pl

use Getopt::Long;

GetOptions ('verbose!' => \$verbose, 'all' => \$all, "catchall" => \$catch);

print "$verbose\n";
print "$all\n";
print "$catch\n";
print "@ARGV\n"
```

In the preceding example, the $verbose variable will be assigned a value of 1 if --verbose is provided as an option and a value of 0 if --noverbose is provided.

To pass arguments to options, use the following syntax:

```perl
#!perl
#long_opt3.pl

use Getopt::Long;

GetOptions ('verbose!' => \$verbose, 'all=i' => \$all, "catchall" => \$catch);

print "$verbose\n";
print "$all\n";
print "$catch\n";
print "@ARGV\n"
```

The "i" means that an integer can be passed. For a string, use "s". For a floating point number, use "f".

You can have multiple values passed in by using the following syntax:

```perl
#!perl
#long_opt4.pl

use Getopt::Long;

 GetOptions ('verbose!' => \$verbose, 'all=i' => \$all, "catchall=s" =>
 \@catch);

print "$verbose\n";
print "$all\n";
print "@catch\n";
print "@ARGV\n"
```

Note that the program would have to be run like this:

```
ocs% perl long_opt4.pl --catch "abc" --catch "xyz"
```

In the following example, you can have users pass key/value pairs to be assigned to a hash:

```perl
#!perl
#long_opt5.pl

use Getopt::Long;
```

```
GetOptions ('verbose!' => \$verbose, 'all=i' => \$all, "catchall=s" =>
\%catch);

print "$catch{test}\n";
print "$catch{error}\n";
print "@ARGV\n"
```

The syntax on the command line would be

```
ocs% perl long_opt5.pl --catch test="abc" --catch error="xyz"
```

There are other options available when you use **Getopt::Long**. Consult the documentation for further details.

Additional resources

In each chapter, resources are provided to provide the learner with a source for more information. These resources may include downloadable source code or links to other books or articles that will provide you more information about the topic at hand.

Resources for this chapter can be found here:

```
https://github.com/Apress/pro-perl-programming
```

Lab exercises

Important note   If you did not finish the previous lab, either finish it before starting this lab or use the completed `parse5.pl` provided in the lab answers folder.

Modify `parse5.pl` to include the following changes:

- Instead of putting the data file in the /tmp directory, place it in the user's home directory. To make it easier to use the HOME environment variable, use the ENV module.

- Prior to displaying the menu, run the command "ps -fe", strip out whitespace as you have done in the past, and store the output in a file called "/tmp/.parse". Compare this new file with parse.txt in the user's home directory. If they are different, ask the user if they want to update their "parse.txt" file with the new file. If the user answers "yes", perform this action. Remove the "/tmp/.parse" file when you are finished.

Save these changes into a file called parse6.pl.

When you have completed your work, compare your script against the parse6.pl file provided in lab answers.

CHAPTER 9

Debugging Tools

A fundamental part of programming is debugging code. This includes not only your own code but often code written by other people. You might be sent some code to debug by a fellow programmer, or download one of the thousands of modules from cpan.org (one which, unfortunately, doesn't work quite as expected).

Fortunately, Perl has a variety of tools to help you debug code. This chapter focuses on many of these tools, including the "warnings" feature, reading diagnostic codes, and the Perl debugger.

Review: The -w switch

Note   The -w switch is discussed in the *Beginning Perl Programming: From Novice to Professional* book. The goal of this section is to provide a quick review of what is covered in that book as well as introduce some additional features of this option.

The -w switch (option) will tell Perl to look for and report unusual (logical errors) code, including the following:

- Variable and filehandle names that are mentioned only once

- Scalar variables that are used before being set

- Redefined subroutines

- References to undefined filehandles

- References to filehandles opened read-only that the script is attempting to write to

© William "Bo" Rothwell of One Course Source, Inc. 2020
W. "Bo" Rothwell, *Pro Perl Programming*, https://doi.org/10.1007/978-1-4842-5605-3_9

- Values used as a number that don't look like numbers

- Subroutines that recurse more than 100 deep

Using the **-w** switch can avoid common (but sometimes tricky) programming errors such as some of the logical error in the following code:

```
#!perl
#w.pl

undef $var;
if ($var == 0) {
  print "yes\n";
}

print GROUP "hello there\n";

$name="Bob";

if ($name == 0) {
    print "yes\n";
}
```

Note that if you ran the previous program, the code would execute without any errors:

```
[student@linux1 student]$  ./w.pl
yes
yes
```

There are, however, problems with this code. The problems are logical in nature, and by using the **-w** option to the **perl** executable, you can see these logical errors:

```
[student@linux1 student]$  perl -w ./w.pl
Name "main::GROUP" used only once: possible typo at w.pl line 9.
Use of uninitialized value $var in numeric eq (==) at w.pl line 5.
yes
print() on unopened filehandle GROUP at w.pl line 9.
Argument "Bob" isn't numeric in numeric eq (==) at w.pl line 13.
yes
```

Note that the code still executed (as demonstrated by the two lines of "yes" output). The **-w** option issues warning messages but does not stop the execution of the code.

The $^W variable

When you use the **-w** switch, the **$^W** variable is set to the value of 1. If you don't use the **-w** switch, the **$^W** variable is set to 0. This is a handy way to see if warnings are turned on at any point in the program. You can also turn warnings on (and off) by modifying this variable.

use warnings

Warnings can also be turned on (and off) with the warnings pragma:

```
use warnings;  #to turn on warnings
no warnings;    #to turn off warnings
```

There are a couple of benefits to using this pragma vs. using the **-w** switch. One advantage is that the **-w** switch turns on "all" warnings, but you can use the pragma to turn on specific warnings:

```
use warning "numeric";
```

Besides "numeric", there are literally dozens of warning categories. See the Category Hierarchy section of warning pragma documentation for more categories of warnings.

The pragma is also scope based, so you can easily turn on (or off) warnings for a chunk of code:

```
use warnings;

{
    no warnings;
    #important code here - warnings off
}
#important code here - warnings on
```

The -W switch

The **-W** switch is like the **-w** switch; however, if you use **-W**, then any attempt to disable warnings in the program will be ignored. This means that **-W** overrides any **no warnings** or **$^W=0** statements, forcing warnings during the entire execution of the program.

This option is useful when you have multiple **no warnings** or **$^W=0** statements in a program and you want to temporarily execute the code with these statements disabled. Instead of commenting out each **no warnings** or **$^W=0** statement, use the **-W** option.

The -X switch

Much like the -W switch, the -X switch will apply to the entire execution of the program. However, the -X switch disables all warnings, regardless if any **use warnings** or **$^W=1** statements exist in the code.

The Perl debugger

Note   Discussed in the *Beginning Perl Programming: From Novice to Professional* book, the goal of this section is to provide a quick review of what is covered in that book as well as introduce some additional powerful features of the Perl debugger.

Perl provides a built-in debugger that can be invoked when running Perl with the **-d** option:

```
[student@linux1 student]$ perl -d use.pl
Loading DB routines from perl5db.pl version 1.0402

Enter h or 'h h' for help

main::(use.pl:2)            copy("example.txt", "newfile.txt ");
  DB<1>
```

Some notes about the debugger:

- Perl must first be able to compile the code prior to entering the debugger.
- `main::(use.pl:2)` means "Main part of script use.pl, line #2".

- At this point, no statements have been executed.

- The command above the prompt (DB<1>) is what the next command to be executed.

Debugger commands

The following chart illustrates the most popular commands available in the debugger:

Command	Meaning
!! cmd	Runs the command (cmd) in a separate process (this is typically a shell command)
b	Create a breakpoint
c	Continue (to next breakpoint)
D	Delete all breakpoints
d	Delete a breakpoint
h	Interactive help
H -num	Prints last "num" Perl statements (excludes debugger commands)
l	Lists the next ten lines of code to be executed
L	List all of the breakpoints and actions
n	Step through a statement (if subroutines are called, executes over the subroutine)
p expr	Essentially the same as Perl's print statement (expr is a Perl expression which can be a value or the outcome of a Perl statement)
q	Quits the debugger
R	Restart the debugger
return	Repeat the last n or s command
S	Lists defined subroutines

(continued)

Command	Meaning
s	Step through a statement (if subroutines are called, executes one subroutine statement at a time)
V [pkg [vars]]	Display all of the variables in package (defaults to main)
x expr	Prints expr in an "easy-to-read" format
y [level [vars]]	Display all of the lexical variables

Getting help

The **h** command brings up a list of debugger commands and a brief description of each. Not much more than the aforementioned list but useful if you don't have this manual handy. The output will scroll off the screen much like a **cat** command in UNIX does. To avoid this, add a pipe character before the command:

```
DB<1> |h
List/search source lines:                      Control script execution:
  l [ln|sub]  List source code                   T            Stack trace
  - or .      List previous/current line  s [expr]    Single step [in expr]
  v [line]    View around line           n [expr]    Next, steps over subs
  f filename  View source in file         <CR/Enter>  Repeat last n or s
  /pattern/ ?patt?    Search forw/backw    r           Return from
                                                        subroutine
  M           Show module versions        c [ln|sub]  Continue until
                                                        position
Debugger controls:                         L           List break/watch/
                                                        actions
  o [...]     Set debugger options        t [n] [expr] Toggle trace [max
                                                         depth] ][trace expr]
  <[<]|{[{]|>[>] [cmd] Do pre/post-prompt b [ln|event|sub] [cnd] Set breakpoint
  ! [N|pat]   Redo a previous command     B ln|*      Delete a/all
                                                        breakpoints
  H [-num]    Display last num commands   a [ln] cmd  Do cmd before line
  = [a val]   Define/list an alias        A ln|*      Delete a/all actions
```

h [db_cmd]	Get help on command	w expr	Add a watch expression
h h	Complete help page	W expr|*	Delete a/all watch exprs
|[|]db_cmd	Send output to pager	![!] syscmd	Run cmd in a subprocess
q or ^D	Quit	R	Attempt a restart

Data Examination: expr   Execute perl code, also see: s,n,t expr

  x|m expr   Evals expr in list context, dumps the result or lists
                    methods.

  p expr   Print expression (uses script's current package).

  S [[!]pat]   List subroutine names [not] matching pattern

  V [Pk [Vars]]   List Variables in Package. Vars can be ~pattern or
                                              !pattern.

  X [Vars]   Same as "V current_package [Vars]". i class inheritance
                                              tree.

  y [n [Vars]]   List lexicals in higher scope <n>. Vars same as V.

  e   Display thread id   E Display all thread ids.

For more help, type h cmd_letter, or run perldoc perldebug for all docs.

Note   The pipe character can be used prior to almost all commands to control scrolling.

An alternative to print

The **x** command provides a more "easy-to-read" method of printing. Its behavior differs greatly depending on the data that it is printing, so you will want to "play with it" to see the differences. A good example to start with is when you print an array:

```
DB<1> @names=qw(red green blue)
DB<2> x @names
0   'red'
1   'green'
2   'blue'
```

Stepping through code

There are two commands that will allow you to step through code: **n** and **s**. Normally, both of these commands work the same: they step through code one step at a time. Where they differ is when you are stepping into a subroutine.

When the **n** command "steps over" a subroutine call, it will execute all of the statements in the subroutine. This is useful when you know that the subroutine is "good" and you don't want to step through each line one at a time.

When the **s** command "steps into" a subroutine call, it will execute each statement in the subroutine one at a time.

Once you have executed a **n** or **s** command, you can re-execute the command again just by pressing the <enter> or <return> keys.

Listing code

To list code, use the **l** command. The **l** command will list a window of lines. Each successive **l** command will show the next ten lines of code to be executed:

```
[student@linux1 student]$  perl -d select.pl
Loading DB routines from perl5db.pl version 1.0402
Emacs support available.
Enter h or `h h' for help.

main::(select.pl:4):  open (LOGFILE, ">/tmp/data${$}$ENV{USER}");
  DB<1> l
4==>     open (LOGFILE, ">/tmp/data${$}$ENV{USER}");
5
6:       print "Starting log\n";  #sends output to STDOUT
7
8:       select LOGFILE;  #output will now go to file
9:       print "Starting log...\n";
10:      print "No errors found\n";
11:      print "End of log\n";
12
13:      select STDOUT;
```

With the **l** command, you can also list either a single line to display or a range of lines:

```
DB<1> l 6
6:      print "Starting log\n";  #sends output to STDOUT
DB<2> l 6-10
6:      print "Starting log\n";  #sends output to STDOUT
7
8:      select LOGFILE;  #output will now go to file
9:      print "Starting log...\n";
10:     print "No errors found\n";
```

Setting breakpoints

The **b** command allows you to set breakpoints. Typically, you set breakpoints at a line number or on a subroutine:

```
DB<1> b 200
DB<2> b test
```

You can also include a conditional statement with the breakpoint:

```
DB<1> b 200 x>100
```

Listing breakpoints

When you create a lot of breakpoints throughout your code, it is sometimes difficult to "see" where the breakpoints are. To see a list of current breakpoints, use the **L** command:

```
 DB<1> b 6
 DB<2> L
4_sleep2.pl:
 6:     for ($i=10;$i>0;$i--) {
   break if (1)
```

Note that when using the **l** command, breakpoints are indicated by a "b" character after the line number (e.g., 5:b):

```
DB<4> l 4-11
4==>      print "countdown!\n\n";
5:b       $|=1;
6:        for ($i=10;$i>0;$i--) {
7:b          print "$i \r";
8:           sleep 1;
9         }
10:       $|=0;
11:b      print "Blast off!\n"
```

Continue to breakpoints

Once breakpoints are set, you can have the debugger execute all code up to the next breakpoint by using the c command:

```
DB<1> b 6
DB<2> c
countdown!

main::(4_sleep2.pl:6):  for ($i=10;$i>0;$i--) {
DB<3>
```

Deleting breakpoints

To delete a breakpoint on a certain line, use the **B** command:

```
DB<1> b 5
DB<2> b 7
DB<3> b 11
DB<4> l 4-11
4==>      print "countdown!\n\n";
5:b       $|=1;
6:        for ($i=10;$i>0;$i--) {
7:b          print "$i \r";
```

```
8:          sleep 1;
9           }
10:         $|=0;
11:b        print "Blast off!\n"
  DB<5> B 5
  DB<6> l 4-11
4==>        print "countdown!\n\n";
5:          $|=1;
6:          for ($i=10;$i>0;$i--) {
7:b            print "$i \r";
8:             sleep 1;
9           }
10:         $|=0;
11:b        print "Blast off!\n"
```

To delete all breakpoints, use the **B *** command:

```
DB<7> B *
Deleting all breakpoints...
DB<8> l 4-11
4==>        print "countdown!\n\n";
5:          $|=1;
6:          for ($i=10;$i>0;$i--) {
7:             print "$i \r";
8:             sleep 1;
9           }
10:         $|=0;
11:         print "Blast off!\n"
12
```

Note   You can also temporary disable a breakpoint with the **disable** command, for example, **disable 7**. To enable a breakpoint again, use the **enable** command: **enable 7**.

Displaying variables and subroutines

The **V** command will display all existing variables in a given package. By default, it displays the variables of the main package:

```
DB<1> V
$@ = ''
FileHandle(stdin) => fileno(0)
%SIG = (
    'ABRT' => undef
{remaining output omitted}
```

Notes

- Most of the output you would normally see has been omitted from the preceding example.

- Normally you want to put the pipe character in front of the V command to control the scrolling of the output.

To display lexical variables, use the **y** command:

```
  DB<1> y
$isa = undef
```

Only lexical variables in the current scope are displayed. If there are higher levels of scope, you can use a numeric value to indicate which level to display: **y 1**

For the **y** command to work correctly, you will likely need to install the PadWalker module. If you are using Strawberry Perl or DWIM Perl or have manually installed the **cpan** client utility, you can execute the following command:

```
cpan PadWalker
```

On ActivePerl, use the following command:

```
ppm install PadWalker
```

To see the currently defined subroutines, use the **S** command:

```
DB<1> S
Carp::carp
```

216

```
Carp::cluck
Carp::confess
Carp::croak
{remaining output omitted}
```

You can limit the output of the **V**, **y**, and **S** commands using regular expressions. For example, to see just the subroutines that have "vars" in the subroutine name, use the following:

```
    DB<2> S vars
Config::config_vars
vars::BEGIN
vars::import
```

Because the pattern can be a regex, you can use syntax like the following:

```
    DB<3> S ^vars
vars::BEGIN
vars::import
```

You can also list all subroutines that don't contain a pattern by placing a ! in front of the regex. For example, **S !^vars** will display all subroutines that don't begin with "vars".

Additional debuggers

The built-in Perl debugger is very powerful; however, there are additional debuggers and debugging features that you may want to explore. The following provides a brief list of some of the more commonly used tools:

- **ActiveState** – ActiveState provides a fork of Perl that includes many useful features (such as ppm to manage Perl modules). ActiveState has a GUI-based debugger which can be used with Komodo IDE, a full IDE for Perl and other languages. Unfortunately, these tools only come with the paid version of ActiveState Perl.

- **Padre, the Perl IDE** – This IDE has some debugging features as well as a host of other features to make finding errors easier.

217

- **Devel:: modules** – This is a large collection of modules that provide useful information that can aid you in debugging scripts. Use the following link to explore: `https://metacpan.org/search?q=Devel%3A%3A&search_type=modules`

Understanding error messages

There are several different categories of error messages. According to the perldiag documentation, "These messages are classified as follows (listed in increasing order of desperation):

> (W) A warning (optional).

> (D) A deprecation (enabled by default).

> (S) A severe warning (enabled by default).

> (F) A fatal error (trappable).

> (P) An internal error you should never see (trappable).

> (X) A very fatal error (nontrappable).

> (A) An alien error message (not generated by Perl)."

The perldiag documentation is an excellent reference for more details regarding specific error messages. There are literally hundreds of messages with explanations provided in this document. For example, consider the following code:

```
#!/usr/bin/perl
#diag1.pl

print "this is only a test;
```

There is a syntax error (no ending quotes), which typically produces the following compiler error:

```
Can't find string terminator ' " ' anywhere before EOF at diag1.pl line 4
```

At this point in your Perl programming experience, this should be a pretty easy problem to diagnose. However, imagine you seeing an error message for the first time. They don't always make 100% sense, so you can use the perldiag page to learn more details. For example, a search for "Can't find string terminator" in the perldiag documentation results in the following:

"Can't find string terminator %s anywhere before EOF

(F) Perl strings can stretch over multiple lines. This message means that the closing delimiter was omitted. Because bracketed quotes count nesting levels, the following is missing its final parenthesis:

        print q(The character '(' starts a side comment.);

If you're getting this error from a here-document, you may have included unseen whitespace before or after your closing tag, or there may not be a linebreak after it. A good programmer's editor will have a way to help you find these characters (or lack of characters). See perlop for the full details on here-documents."

use diagnostics

The diagnostics pragma will use the content of perldiag to provide more verbose error messages. This statement is very useful when debugging programs; consider the following code:

```
#!/usr/bin/perl
#diag2.pl

use diagnostics;
print "this is only a test;
```

There is a syntax error (no ending quotes), which typically produces the following compiler error:

```
Can't find string terminator ' " ' anywhere before EOF at diag2.pl line 5
```

When run when diagnostics are "turned on", the following error is displayed:

```
Can't find string terminator '"' anywhere before EOF at diag2.pl line 5 (#1)
```

(F) Perl strings can stretch over multiple lines. This message
means   that the closing delimiter was omitted. Because
bracketed quotes count nesting levels, the following is missing
its final parenthesis:

```
    print q(The character '(' starts a side comment.);
```

If you're getting this error from a here-document, you may have
included unseen whitespace before or after your closing tag or
there may not be a linebreak after it. A good programmer's editor
will have a way to help you find these characters (or lack of
characters). See perlop for the full details on here-documents.

Uncaught exception from user code:
```
    Can't find string terminator '"' anywhere before EOF at diag2.pl
    line 5.
```

Carp

The Carp module can be used to generate error messages. The module provides functions that act similar to Perl's **warn** and **die** commands:

Function	Purpose
Carp	Produces error messages similar to warn
Croak	Acts similar to the die statement

Using carp

The built-in Perl statement **warn** will print error messages to STDERR. It will also display the line number in which the error occurred.

The **carp** command will perform in the same manner in cases in which it is called within the main part of the program. If it is called within a subroutine, it will also provide the original line from where the subroutine was called:

```perl
#!perl
#carp.pl

use Carp;

sub warnings {
    warn "This is warn with a newline char\n";
    warn "This is what warn look like";
    carp "This is what carp looks like";
}

&warnings;
```

Output of the preceding program:

```
[student@linux1 student]$  ./carp.pl
This is warn with a newline char
This is what warn look like at ./carp.pl line 8.
This is what carp looks like at ./carp.pl line 9.
        main::warnings called at ./carp.pl line 12
```

Using croak

The built-in Perl statement **die** will print error messages to STDERR and exit your script. It will also display the line number in which the error occurred.

The **croak** statement will perform in the same manner in cases in which it is called within the main part of the program. If it is called within a subroutine, it will also provide the original line from where the subroutine was called:

```perl
#!perl
#die.pl

sub finish {
    die "This is what die looks like";
}
```

```perl
&finish;

print "Never will get to here";
```

Sample output of the preceding **die** example:

```
[student@linux1 student]$  ./die.pl
This is what die looks like at ./die.pl line 5.
```

```perl
#!perl
#croak.pl

use Carp;

sub finish {
    croak "This is what croak looks like";
}

&finish;

print "Never will get to here";
```

Sample output of the above **croak** example:

```
[student@linux1 student]$  ./croak.pl
This is what croak looks like at ./croak.pl line 7
        main::finish called at ./croak.pl line 10
```

Data::Dumper

Remember back to the Perl debugger when you used the **x** command to print data in a "nicer" format:

```
DB<1> @names=qw(red green blue)
DB<2> x @names
0  'red'
1  'green'
2  'blue'
```

When you use the **x** command, it uses the Data::Dumper module to format the output. You can use this module to print data from within your script:

```perl
#!perl
#dump.pl

use Data::Dumper;

print Dumper (\%ENV);
```

Note   The "\" before %ENV is used to make a reference to the %ENV hash.

```perl
$Data::Dumper::Indent = 0;
$Data::Dumper::Useqq = 1;
$Data::Dumper::Terse = 1;
$Data::Dumper::Sortkeys = 1;
```

Perl style

While style (the format of your code) isn't really a debugging "feature", a poorly formatted program does make it more difficult to debug. You should at the very least pick a style and be consistent throughout the program. Consider reading the perlstyle documentation guide for some good suggestions on good policies to follow. Here are just a few of the suggestions offered in the perlstyle guide:

- Four-column indent.

- Opening curly on same line as keyword, if possible; otherwise, line up.

- Space before the opening curly of a multiline BLOCK.

- One-line BLOCK may be put on one line, including curlies.

- No space before the semicolon.

Additional resources

In each chapter, resources are provided to provide the learner with a source for more information. These resources may include downloadable source code or links to other books or articles that will provide you more information about the topic at hand.

Resources for this chapter can be found here:

```
https://github.com/Apress/pro-perl-programming
```

Lab exercises

Important note   If you did not finish the previous lab, either finish it before starting this lab or use the completed `parse6.pl` provided in the lab answers folder.

Modify `parse6.pl` to include the following changes:

- Take some time to get familiar with the capacities of the Perl debugger.

- Use the -w switch to have Perl look for logical errors.

- Implement "`use diagnostics`" to have verbose error message displayed.

- Replace your die and warn statements with croak and carp statements.

Save these changes into a file called `parse7.pl`.

When you have completed your work, compare your script against the `parse7.pl` file provided in lab answers.

CHAPTER 10

Perl/TK Basics

The idea behind Tk is to create an easy-to-use interface between Perl and Windows. In order to do this, Tk builds on top of the X Window System (or Microsoft Windows) to create "sub-windows" that contain buttons, menu bars, scroll bars, and other windows components. These components are called *widgets*.

Widgets are controls that are built into Motif (the heart of the X Window System on UNIX platforms). In fact, you can think of Tk as the process of putting widgets together in an application until you have the graphic interface you need.

The TK module

TK isn't part of Perl by default. It needs to be installed on your system and imported into your program with the **use** statement.

To determine if TK is installed on your system, run the following command:

```
perl -e "use Tk;"
```

If you don't get any error messages, Tk is installed. If you do get an error message, like the one displayed here, Tk is probably not installed:

```
perl -e "use Tk;"
Can't locate Tk.pm in @INC (you may need to install the Tk module) (@INC
contains: C:/Strawberry/perl/site/lib C:/Strawberry/perl/vendor/lib C:/
Strawberry/perl/lib) at -e line 1.
BEGIN failed--compilation aborted at -e line 1.
```

If the TK module is not installed and you are using Strawberry Perl or DWIM Perl or have manually installed the **cpan** client utility, you can execute the following command:

```
cpan Tk
```

225

© William "Bo" Rothwell of One Course Source, Inc. 2020
W. "Bo" Rothwell, *Pro Perl Programming*, https://doi.org/10.1007/978-1-4842-5605-3_10

On ActivePerl, use the following command:

```
ppm install Tk
```

Important note   Tk is a huge topic. While this section will show you how to create and use basic widgets, a complete discussion of Tk is beyond the scope of this book.

Types of widgets

The following are the primary widgets available to Tk:

Widget	Purpose
Frames	Used to group other widgets together
Toplevels	Toplevels are special frames that create a "separate" window (not a sub-window like normal frames do)
Labels	Similar to frames but also allow text and bitmap graphics to be displayed
Buttons	Buttons can be used to *bind* an action to a graphic
Checkbuttons	Used to select options
Radiobuttons	Used to select one option only
Listboxes	Lists lines of text and allows user to select one or more line
Scroll bars	Allows the user to control the display with a scroll bar
Scales	Allows the user to control the setting of an item with a slider bar
Entries	Allows the user to type in text
Menus	Give the user menu options

Each of these widgets will be discussed in greater detail in the next chapter.

> **A note regarding options:** There are many options for widgets that affect size, position, effects, and additional widget features. Many of these options will be discussed as the widgets are explored.

Exploring widget examples

In addition to the examples provided in this book, there are some examples that are included with the TK module itself. These examples can be very useful in learning about how TK works.

To access these examples, you first need to discover the location of where the TK module is. This can be done by executing the following statements in the Perl debugger:

```
DB<1> use Tk
```

```
DB<2> print $INC{"Tk.pm"}
C:/Strawberry/perl/site/lib/Tk.pm
```

At the same level as the `"perl"` directory, there should be a `"cpan"` directory and subdirectories under this as shown here:

```
C:\Strawberry\cpan\build\Tk-804.034-0\demos
```

In the demos directory, there are several examples that show you how TK works. Start by reading the README file. You will likely find the **widget** program most useful at first:

```
C:\Strawberry\cpan\build\Tk-804.034-0\demos> perl widget
```

```
🦞 Perl/Tk Widget Demonstration                    —    ☐    ✕

File   Help
```

Perl/Tk Widget Demonstrations

This application provides a front end for several short scripts that demonstrate what you can do with Tk widgets. Each of the numbered lines below describes a demonstration; you can click on it to invoke the demonstration. Once the demonstration window appears, you can click the **See Code** button to see the Perl/Tk code that created the demonstration. If you wish, you can edit the code and click the **Rerun Demo** button in the code window to reinvoke the demonstration with the modified code.

Getting Started
1. An introduction to Perl/Tk.

Labels, buttons, checkbuttons, and radiobuttons
1. Labels (text and images).
2. Labels and Unicode text.
3. Buttons.
4. Checkbuttons (select any of a group).
5. Radiobuttons (select one of a group).
6. A 15-puzzle game made out of buttons.
7. Iconic buttons that use bitmaps.
8. Two labels displaying images.
9. A simple user interface for viewing images.
10. Labelled frames.

Listboxes
1. The 50 states.
2. Change widget's color scheme.

Each link (colored in blue) represents a small example program. For example, if you click the "1. Labels (text and images)." link, another program will launch like the following:

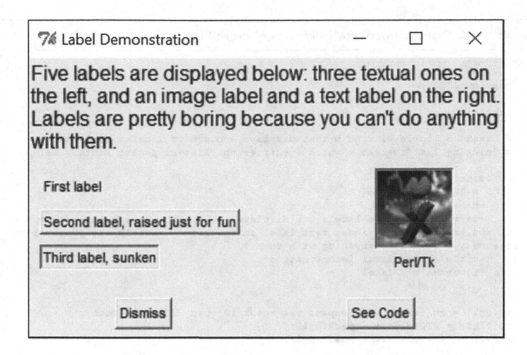

For each of these example programs, there is a "See Code" button that you can use to see the code that created the TK program. For example, if you click the "See Code" button for the "Label Demonstration" program, you would see the following.

```
7% Demo code: C:/Strawberry/perl/site/lib/Tk/demos/widget_lib/labels.pl          —    □    ✕

# labels.pl

use vars qw/$TOP/;

sub labels {

    # Create a top-level window that displays a bunch of labels.  @pl is the
    # "packing list" variable which specifies the list of packer attributes.

    my($demo) = @_;
    $TOP = $MW->WidgetDemo(
        -name     => $demo,
        -text     => 'Five labels are displayed below: three textual ones on the
 left, and an image label and a text label on the right.  Labels are pretty bori
ng because you can\'t do anything with them.',
        -title    => 'Label Demonstration',
        -iconname => 'label',
    );

    my(@pl) = qw/-side left -expand yes -padx 10 -pady 10 -fill both/;
    my $left = $TOP->Frame->pack(@pl);
    my $right = $TOP->Frame->pack(@pl);

    @pl = qw/-side top -expand yes -pady 2 -anchor w/;
    my $left_l1 = $left->Label(-text => 'First label')->pack(@pl);
    my $left_l2 = $left->Label(
        -text   => 'Second label, raised just for fun',
        -relief => 'raised',
    )->pack(@pl);
    my $left_l3 = $left->Label(
        -text   => 'Third label, sunken',
        -relief => 'sunken',
    )->pack(@pl);

    @pl = qw/-side top/;
    my $right_bitmap = $right->Label(
        -image       => $TOP->Photo(-file => Tk->findINC('Xcamel.gif')),
        -borderwidth => 2,
        -relief      => 'sunken',
    )->pack(@pl);

                Dismiss                                      Rerun Demo
```

Try it!

Perform the following steps:

- Try running the different programs that are provided by the widget demo program. Don't worry about the code details, but rather focus on the features that are available for Perl TK (buttons, listboxes, etc.).

- Try some of the other programs that are mentioned in the README file. Some of the more interesting ones are listed here:

  - ixset

  - rolodex

  - timer

Geometry managers

While you can modify the look and feel of widgets with different options, geometry managers control the location and size of widgets. Consider these managers as functions that can see the "big picture", while the widgets only can see themselves.

The primary geometry manager in Tk is **pack**. This manager can place a series of widgets within a frame. The **pack** geometry manager is useful for simple Tk applications.

The **grid** geometry manager is designed to allow you to place widgets into rows and columns. The **place** geometry manager is designed to place widgets using an x/y coordinate.

The **pack** geometry manager is probably the most commonly used of the three and the easiest to initially learn. As a result, this book will focus on the **pack** geometry manager.

Creating widgets

To get started, we are going to create a very simple Tk script. The following will just create a window:

```perl
#!perl
#basic.pl

use Tk;

$main = MainWindow -> new;
$main -> title ("First Tk program!");
MainLoop;
```

Notes about the program:

- The "use Tk;" statement imports the Tk module.

- The line "$main = MainWindow -> new;" tells Tk that you want to create a window. The window isn't created until you run the "MainLoop" statement.

- The line "$main -> title ("First Tk program!");" tells Tk that you want to put the string "First Tk program!" in the title bar of the window.

- The line "MainLoop;" creates the window. This statement is referred to as an "event loop".

The OO nature of the Tk module

One aspect of Perl/Tk that "throws" people is that it is an object-oriented module. If you don't know how OO works in Perl, don't let this aspect of the module throw you off. The good thing about object-oriented programming in Perl is that you don't have to understand how to write or read OO Perl code in order to use an OO module.

If you understand the concept of OO from other languages (such as C++ or Java), then the following might be useful information:

```perl
$main = MainWindow -> new;
```

This command calls the "new" method from the "MainWindow" class and returns an object that is assigned to the $main variable.

With that said, understand that OOP is a concept, not a standard; therefore, how OOP "works" in C++ or Java can be quite a bit different than how it works in Perl.

Once again, since you don't know how to write or read OO code in order to use an OO module, covering more detail regarding OOP in Perl is deferred to another book.

Additional resources

In each chapter, resources are provided to provide the learner with a source for more information. These resources may include downloadable source code or links to other books or articles that will provide you more information about the topic at hand.

Resources for this chapter can be found here:

```
https://github.com/Apress/pro-perl-programming
```

Lab exercises

Important note   If you did not finish the previous lab, either finish it before starting this lab or use the completed parse7.pl provided in the lab answers folder.

Taking an existing command-line-based script and converting it into a GUI-based script can be challenging. Typically, the best course of action is to create a separate GUI-based script and incorporate the code from the command-line-based script.

To start this process, create a program that will generate a window that has the title of "Process Data". At this point the program shouldn't do anything except provide a window. Do not attempt to include the code from parse7.pl at this time!

Save this program as parse8.pl.

When you have completed your work, compare your script against the parse7.pl file provided in lab answers.

CHAPTER 11

Perl TK Widgets

The heart of TK are the widgets. Widgets are window-based components that allow the user to interact with the program. This chapter will focus on some of the more commonly used Perl TK widgets, but keep in mind that there are additional, often more advanced, widgets that you can explore on your own if you decide that you want to make some more advanced TK-based programs.

Frames

Frames are great for creating sub-windows within your primary window and grouping other widgets. To create a frame, use the following syntax:

```
$frame = $main ->Frame ([option => value, ...]) ->pack;
```

or:

```
$frame = $main ->Frame ([option => value, ...]);
$frame ->pack;
```

Recall that the **pack** command places the widget into a window (or a toplevel or frame). In the first example, the widget is placed into the $main window as it is created. In the second, the widget is placed into the $main window after it is created.

If the **pack** command occurs directly after the widget is defined, then there isn't any difference between these two techniques. However, you can define a widget at any time and then pack it later. In most cases, however, you will want to pack the widget at the same time you define it.

Note You don't have to pack the main window (or toplevels).

© William "Bo" Rothwell of One Course Source, Inc. 2020
W. "Bo" Rothwell, *Pro Perl Programming*, https://doi.org/10.1007/978-1-4842-5605-3_11

Relief

The **-relief** option allows you to specify a 3-D border. The following chart lists the different relief options that are available:

- raised • sunken • flat
- groove • ridge

relief example

```
#!perl
#relief.pl
use Tk;

$main = MainWindow -> new;
$frame1 = $main -> Frame (-relief => raised, -height => 150, -width => 200,
                                            -borderwidth => 15) ->pack;

$frame2 = $main -> Frame (-relief => sunken, -height => 150, -width => 200,
                                            -borderwidth => 15) ->pack;

$frame3 = $main -> Frame (-relief => flat, -height => 150, -width => 200,
                                            -borderwidth => 15) ->pack;

$frame4 = $main -> Frame (-relief => groove, -height => 150, -width => 200,
                                            -borderwidth => 15) ->pack;

$frame5 = $main -> Frame (-relief => ridge, -height => 150, -width => 200,
                                            -borderwidth => 15) ->pack;

MainLoop;
```

Notes about the **relief.pl**

- The **-height** and **-width** options tell the **pack** command how large (in pixels) to make the frame.

- The **-borderwidth** option tells the **pack** command how large (in pixels) to make the border.

- Don't forget to specify a borderwidth and a size (height and width). Without these options, **pack** will not assign a border to the frame, and the **-relief** option does nothing.

- More details on sizes (height, width, borderwidth, etc.) will be discussed in a later section.

Output of relief.pl:

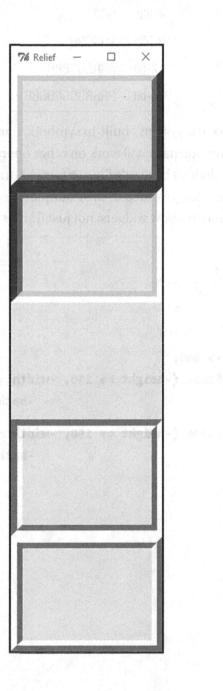

Colors

When specifying colors for options such as -background, you can either use "red, green, blue" (RGB) component syntax or use the system's built-in symbolic name. The RGB can be specified either in 4-bit, 8-bit, 12-bit, or 16-bit:

4-bit:	RGB
8-bit:	RRGGBB
12-bit:	RRRGGGBBB
16-bit	RRRRGGGGBBBB

For UNIX and Linux, the system's built-in symbolic names are listed in the file "rgb.txt". These names normally will work on other operating systems as well. In the event that your system doesn't have this file, perform an Internet search for "rgb.txt". There is also a "rgb.txt" file provided in the examples for this book.

Colors can be applied to many widgets, not just frames as shown in the next example.

Color example:

```perl
#!perl
#colors.pl

use Tk;

$main = MainWindow -> new;
$frame1 = $main -> Frame (-height => 150, -width => 200,
                                        -background => red) ->pack;

$frame2 = $main -> Frame (-height => 150, -width => 200,
                                        -background => blue) ->pack;

MainLoop;
```

Output of `colors.pl`:

Labels

Labels are used to display text and bitmaps. To create a label, use the following syntax:

```
$label = $main ->Label ([option => value, ...]) ->pack;
```

bitmaps

You can display either internally defined bitmaps or external bitmaps. The following lists
the different internal bitmaps available:

• error	• gray50	• info	• question
• gray25	• hourglass	• questhead	• warning
• gray12	• gray75	• k	• transparent

Note   The widgets demo program includes code to display all of the internal bitmaps (look under "Miscellaneous" for The built-in bitmaps):

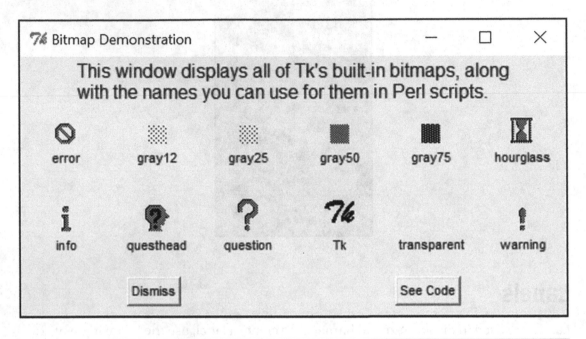

To display an external bitmap, place a "@" character before the path to the file. Example using internal bitmap:

```perl
#!perl
#bitmap1.pl

use Tk;

$main = MainWindow -> new;
$label = $main -> Label (-bitmap => 'questhead') -> pack;
MainLoop;
```

Output of `bitmap1.pl`:

Example using external bitmap:

```perl
#!perl
#bitmap2.pl

use Tk;

$main = MainWindow -> new;
$label= $main -> Label (-bitmap =>
                                    '@Toronto.bm')
                                    -> pack;

MainLoop;
```

Using other images

A bitmap image can be directly "recognized" by Tk. To use other images, you can use another tool to covert the image to a bitmap, or use the **-image** option. To use the **-image** option, you first need to create an "image pointer" by using the **Photo** statement.

Example using a gif image:

```perl
#!perl
#image.pl

use Tk;

$main = MainWindow -> new;
$image = $main -> Photo(-file => "activeperl_logo.gif");
$label = $main -> Label (-image => $image) -> pack;
MainLoop;
```

Output of image.pl:

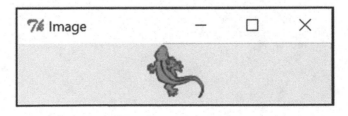

text

You can display text inside a label by using the **-text** option. The **-font** option can be used to define the font of the text that is displayed in the label widget.

The format of the font is as follows:

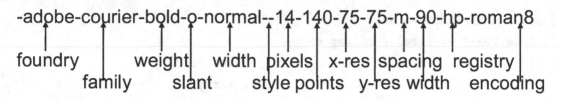

To list all of the fonts available on a Unix or Linux system, run the **xlsfonts** command. Font example:

```perl
#!perl
#fonts1.pl

use Tk;

$main = MainWindow -> new;
$lab1 = $main -> Label (
          -text => "Perl is the best",
          -font => '-adobe-courier-medium-o-normal--24-240-75-75-m-150-hp-
          roman8') -> pack;
$lab2 = $main -> Label (
          -text => "Don't you think?",
          -font => '-adobe-helvetica-medium-o-normal--24-240-75-75-p-130-
          iso8859-1') -> pack;

MainLoop;
```

Output of fonts1.pl:

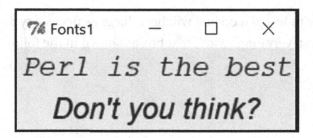

Note that you don't need to provide the complete font definition. For example, the following program defines just the foundry and family:

```perl
#!perl
#fonts2.pl

use Tk;

$main = MainWindow -> new;
$lab1 = $main -> Label (
          -text => "Perl is the best",
          -font => '-adobe-courier') -> pack;
$lab2 = $main -> Label (
          -text => "Don't you think?",
          -font => '-adobe-helvetica') -> pack;
MainLoop;
```

Output of fonts2.pl:

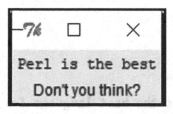

Text wrapping

By default, a label with text placed in it will be as large as necessary to fit the text within it. This may result in a very long (wide) text box as shown in the following example:

```perl
#!perl
#wrap1.pl

use Tk;

$main = MainWindow -> new;
$lab1 = $main -> Label (
          -text => "Perl is the best language for performing actions such a
          s text filtering.",
           -font =>
             '-adobe-courier-medium-o-normal--24-240-75-75-m-150-hp-roman8')
             -> pack;

MainLoop;
```

   Output of wrap1.pl:

```
Wrap1                                                             —   □   ×
Perl is the best language for performing actions such as text filtering.
```

   You can use the **-wraplength** option to specify how long each line of text should be:

```perl
#!perl
#wrap2.pl

use Tk;

$main = MainWindow -> new;
$lab1 = $main -> Label (
          -text => "Perl is the best language for performing actions such
          as text filtering.",
          -font => '-adobe-courier-medium-o-normal--24-240-75-75-m-150-hp-
          roman8',
          -wraplength => 200) -> pack;

MainLoop;
```

Output of `wrap2.pl`:

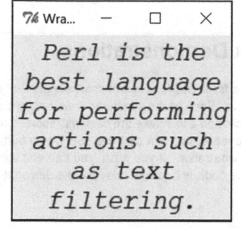

Try it!

Perform the following steps:

- Open the widget program from the demos directory (this was covered in Chapter 10).

- Review the programs and the source code of the following:

  - Labels (text and images)

  - Labels and Unicode text

  - Two labels displaying images

7k Perl/Tk Widget Demonstration   —   □   ×

File   Help

Perl/Tk Widget Demonstrations

This application provides a front end for several short scripts that demonstrate what you can do with Tk widgets. Each of the numbered lines below describes a demonstration; you can click on it to invoke the demonstration. Once the demonstration window appears, you can click the **See Code** button to see the Perl/Tk code that created the demonstration. If you wish, you can edit the code and click the **Rerun Demo** button in the code window to reinvoke the demonstration with the modified code.

Getting Started
1. An introduction to Perl/Tk.

Labels, buttons, checkbuttons, and radiobuttons
1. Labels (text and images).
2. Labels and Unicode text.
3. Buttons.
4. Checkbuttons (select any of a group).
5. Radiobuttons (select one of a group).
6. A 15-puzzle game made out of buttons.
7. Iconic buttons that use bitmaps.
8. Two labels displaying images.
9. A simple user interface for viewing images.
10. Labelled frames.

Listboxes
1. The 50 states.
2. Change widget's color scheme.

Buttons

Buttons are useful for assigning a command to a widget and to set variables. There are three types of buttons:

Button	Purpose
Button	When a user clicks a button, a command (subroutine) will be run
Checkbutton	Allows the user to select multiple items from a list of items
Radiobutton	Allows the user to select one item from a list of items

Button example

```perl
#!perl
#button.pl

use Tk;

sub info {$lab1 = $main -> Label (-bitmap => 'info') -> pack;}
sub error {$lab2 = $main -> Label (-bitmap => 'error') -> pack;}
sub warning {$lab3 = $main -> Label (-bitmap => 'warning') -> pack;}

$main = MainWindow -> new;
$but1 = $main -> Button (
        -text => "Show info",
        -command => sub {&info}) -> pack;
$but2 = $main -> Button (
        -text => "Show error",
        -command => sub {&error}) -> pack;
$but3 = $main -> Button (
        -text => "Show warning",
        -command => sub {&warning}) -> pack;

MainLoop;
```

247

Notes about the program

- The **-text** option allows you to specify what text you want displayed in the button.

- The **-command** option allows you to specify what statement or subroutine to execute if the user clicks the button. This can be a set of Perl statements enclosed with the curly braces, but most often it will be a reference to a function call.

Output of `button.pl`:

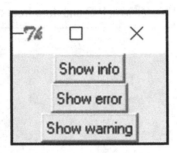

Using buttons to exit your script

Buttons can be used allow the user to exit the application. The following example shows how this can be done:

```perl
#!perl
#exit.pl

use Tk;

sub info {$lab1 = $main -> Label (-bitmap => 'info') -> pack;}
sub error {$lab2 = $main -> Label (-bitmap => 'error') -> pack;}
sub warning {$lab3 = $main -> Label (-bitmap => 'warning') -> pack;}

$main = MainWindow -> new;
$but1 = $main -> Button (
        -text => "Show info",
        -command => sub {&info}) -> pack;
$but2 = $main -> Button (
        -text => "Show error",
        -command => sub {&error}) -> pack;
```

```perl
$but3 = $main -> Button (
          -text => "Show warning",
          -command => sub {&warning}) -> pack;
$but4 = $main -> Button (
          -text => "Exit",
          -command => sub {exit}) -> pack;

MainLoop;
```

Using buttons to destroy widgets

The action that is taken when a button is pressed can also include destroying a widget.
This example shows how to do this and also demonstrates how to modify an existing
widget with the **configure** option.

```perl
#!perl
#dest.pl

use Tk;

sub info_remove {
    $lab1 -> destroy;
    $but1 -> configure (
            -text => "Show info",
            -command => sub {&info});
}

sub info {
    $lab1 = $main -> Label (-bitmap => 'info') -> pack;
    $but1 -> configure (
            -text => "Remove info",
            -command => sub {&info_remove});
}

$main = MainWindow -> new;
$but1 = $main -> Button (
          -text => "Show info",
          -command => sub {&info}) -> pack;
```

```
$but2 = $main -> Button (
        -text => "Exit",
        -command => sub {exit}) -> pack;
```

```
MainLoop;
```

Output of dest.pl when initially executed:

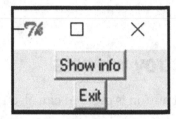

Output of dest.pl after "Show info" button is pressed:

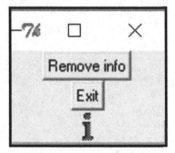

Output of dest.pl after "Remove info" button is pressed:

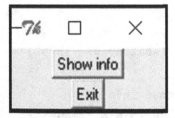

Unpacking instead of destroying

Using **destroy** will not only remove your widget from the window, but it will also
"delete" the contents of the variable that stored the widget. This means you would need
to recreate the widget if you want to use it again.

If you want to remove the widget from a window, but also want to use the widget again, use the **packForget** operation:

```perl
$lab1 -> packForget();
```

Changing the cursor

Within most widgets, including buttons, you can modify the look of the cursor by using the **-cursor** option:

```perl
#!perl
#cursor.pl

use Tk;

sub info_remove {
    $top -> destroy;
    $but1 -> configure (
                                    -text => "Show info",
                                    -command => sub {&info});
}

sub info {
    $lab1 = $main -> Label (-bitmap => 'info') -> pack;
    $but1 -> configure (
                                    -text => "Remove info",
                                    -command => sub {&info_remove});
}

$main = MainWindow -> new;
$but1 = $main -> Button (
                                        -text => "Show info",
                                        -command => sub {&info},
                                        -cursor => hand2) -> pack;
$but2 = $main -> Button (-text => "Exit",
                                        -command => sub {exit},
                                        -cursor => X_cursor) -> pack;

MainLoop;
```

Note   Try running the previous program and then point your mouse icon to each button.

Opening a toplevel

Toplevels are just like frames. You can use them to organize and "hold" other widgets. While frames reside within the primary window, toplevels are used to create another window, "separate" from the primary window.

A few other points about toplevels:

- Toplevels are very useful for dialog boxes.

- If you destroy the default window, the toplevel window will also be destroyed.

Toplevel example:

```perl
#!perl
#top.pl

use Tk;

sub info_remove {
    $lab1 -> destroy;
    $but1 -> configure (-text => "Show info", -command => sub {&info});
}

sub info {
    $top = $main -> Toplevel();
    $lab1 = $top -> Label (-bitmap => 'info') -> pack;
    $but1 -> configure (-text => "Remove info", -command => sub {&info_remove});
}

$main = MainWindow -> new;
$but1 = $main -> Button (-text => "Show info", -command => sub {&info}) -> pack;
$but2 = $main -> Button (-text => "Exit", -command => sub {exit}) -> pack;

MainLoop;
```

Output of `top.pl` when program starts:

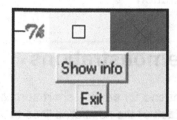

Output of `top.pl` after clicking the "`Show info`" button:

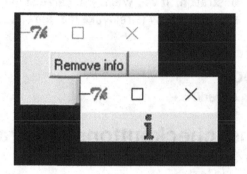

 **Try it!**

Perform the following steps:

- Open the widget program from the demos directory (this was covered in Chapter 10).

- Review the programs and the source code of the following:

  - Buttons

  - A 15-puzzle game made out of buttons

  - Iconic buttons that use bitmaps

```
🦴 Perl/Tk Widget Demonstration              —   ☐    ✕

File   Help
```

Perl/Tk Widget Demonstrations

This application provides a front end for several short scripts that demonstrate what you can do with Tk widgets. Each of the numbered lines below describes a demonstration; you can click on it to invoke the demonstration. Once the demonstration window appears, you can click the **See Code** button to see the Perl/Tk code that created the demonstration. If you wish, you can edit the code and click the **Rerun Demo** button in the code window to reinvoke the demonstration with the modified code.

Getting Started

    1. An introduction to Perl/Tk.

Labels, buttons, checkbuttons, and radiobuttons

    1. Labels (text and images).
    2. Labels and Unicode text.
    3. Buttons.
    4. Checkbuttons (select any of a group).
    5. Radiobuttons (select one of a group).
    6. A 15-puzzle game made out of buttons.
    7. Iconic buttons that use bitmaps.
    8. Two labels displaying images.
    9. A simple user interface for viewing images.
    10. Labelled frames.

Listboxes

    1. The 50 states.
    2. Change widget's color scheme.

Lab

Important note   If you did not finish the previous lab, either finish it before starting this lab or use the completed `parse8.pl` provided in the lab answers folder.

Using code from `parse7.pl` and `parse8.pl`, generate a script that will perform the following operation:

- Determine if the parse.txt file in the user's home directory is up to date. If not, use a toplevel to ask the user if they want an updated file. You should incorporate the code from the `parse7.pl` script to perform the non-GUI aspects of this program. Don't worry about the position of the toplevel for now.

- Read the data from the user's parse.txt file into the @proc variable.

Store these changes in a file called `parse9-1.pl`.

When you have completed your work, compare your script against the `parse9-1.pl` file provided in lab answers.

Checkbuttons

With checkbuttons users can turn on and off values. You can assign actions for "on" values and "off" values. The following is a modification of `button.pl` using checkbuttons:

```
#!perl
#check.pl

use Tk;

sub info {$lab1 = $main -> Label (-bitmap => 'info') -> pack;}
sub rminfo {$lab1 -> destroy;}

$main = MainWindow -> new;
$but1 = $main -> Checkbutton (-text => "Show info",
                                      -variable => \$info,
                                      -command => sub {
                                      if ($info) {
                                      &info
                                      }
                                      else {
                                      &rminfo;
                                      }}) -> pack;

MainLoop;
```

255

Notes about the program:

- The **-variable** option allows you to assign a value of 0 or 1 to a variable.

- If the user "turns on" the checkbox by clicking it, the value of the variable is set to 1.

- If the user "turns off" the checkbox by clicking it, the value of the variable is set to 0

- The \ character before the variable name is so Perl accesses the variable as a reference.

- The **-command** option allows you to execute a statement or subroutine based on the user's action.

Output of check.pl when program starts:

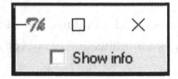

Output of check.pl after clicking the check box:

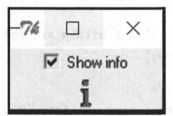

Radiobuttons

With checkbuttons, you can select more than one option. With Radiobuttons, you can only select one option from a group of options:

```perl
#!perl
#radio.pl

use Tk;

$main = MainWindow -> new;
$but1 = $main -> Radiobutton (-text => "Show info",
                                        -value => "info",
                                        -variable => \$setting)
                                        -> pack;
$but2 = $main -> Radiobutton (-text => "Show error",
                                        -value => "error",
                                        -variable => \$setting)
                                        -> pack;
$but3 = $main -> Radiobutton (-text => "Show warning",
                                        -value => "warn",
                                        -variable => \$setting)
                                        -> pack;

MainLoop;
```

When a user checks an option, its "value" is set to the variable. For example, if a user were to check "Show info", the value of the $setting variable would be set to "info".

Output of radio.pl:

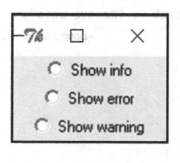

Padding

You can use the **-padx** and -**pady** options to "pad" the borders of a widget. Padding is good for creating nice-looking formats.

Padding (and other "size" options such as **-width** and **-height**) can be accomplished by several different units:

- Centimeters – "c"

- Inches – "i"

- Millimeters – "m"

- Points – "p"

If you don't specify a unit type, pixels are assumed by default.

Padding example:

```perl
#!perl
#pad.pl

use Tk;

sub info_remove {
    $top -> destroy;
    $but1 -> configure (-text => "Show info",
                                        -command => sub {&info});
}

sub info {
    $top = $main -> Toplevel();
    $lab1 = $top -> Label (-bitmap => 'info',) -> pack;
    $but1 -> configure (-text => "Remove info",
                                        -command => sub {&info_remove});
}
```

```
$main = MainWindow -> new;
$but1 = $main -> Button (-text => "Show info",
                                    -padx => 50,
                                    -pady => 25,
                                    -command => sub {&info}) -> pack;
$but2 = $main -> Button (-text => "Exit",
                                         -command => sub {exit}) -> pack;

MainLoop;
```

Output of pad.pl:

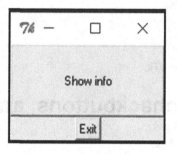

Try it!

Perform the following steps:

- Open the widget program from the demos directory (this was covered in Chapter 10).

- Review the programs and the source code of the following:

  - Checkbuttons (select any of a group)

  - Radiobuttons (select one of a group)

7⁄6 Perl/Tk Widget Demonstration   —   □   ✕

File   Help

Perl/Tk Widget Demonstrations

This application provides a front end for several short scripts that demonstrate what
you can do with Tk widgets. Each of the numbered lines below describes a
demonstration; you can click on it to invoke the demonstration. Once the
demonstration window appears, you can click the **See Code** button to see the Perl/Tk
code that created the demonstration. If you wish, you can edit the code and click the
Rerun Demo button in the code window to reinvoke the demonstration with the
modified code.

Getting Started
  1. An introduction to Perl/Tk.

Labels, buttons, checkbuttons, and radiobuttons
  1. Labels (text and images).
  2. Labels and Unicode text.
  3. Buttons.
  4. Checkbuttons (select any of a group).
  5. Radiobuttons (select one of a group).
  6. A 15-puzzle game made out of buttons.
  7. Iconic buttons that use bitmaps.
  8. Two labels displaying images.
  9. A simple user interface for viewing images.
  10. Labelled frames.

Listboxes
  1. The 50 states.
  2. Change widget's color scheme.

Listboxes

Listboxes will display a collection of strings of which the user can select one or more. To
create a listbox, use the following syntax:

```
$lb = $main ->Listbox ([option => value, ...]) ->pack;
```

Listbox example:

```perl
#!perl
#list1.pl

use Tk;

open (COLORS, "<rgb.txt") || die;

$temp=<COLORS>;  #need to remove 1st line

$main = MainWindow -> new;
$lb = $main -> Listbox  -> pack;
while (<COLORS>) {
    chomp;
    s/^[0123456789 ]+//;
    s/\t\t//;
    $lb -> insert('end', $_);
}

MainLoop;
```

In this example, we created a Listbox with the following statement: **$lb = $main ->**
Listbox -> pack;

To add items to the Listbox, the **$lb -> insert('end', $_);** line was used. These
items came from data in the **rgb.txt** file.

Output of list1.pl:

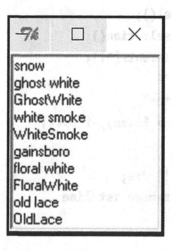

Notes about the program:

- If you look at the **rbg.txt** file, you will notice that there are more than ten colors in the file. What happened to the remaining colors?

- Click any color in the list box, hold down the mouse, and scroll down. More colors will appear.

- This isn't a very "user-friendly" way of displaying lists; scrollbars will be added soon to make it easier to see all of the items.

Using selected values

You can determine what the user selected in a Listbox by using the **curselection** function. Since the user can select more than one item in a Listbox, this function returns a list of values that indicate the item(s) that the user has selected.

The list returned by the **curselection** function is not the actual item that was selected but rather the index positions of the items. To determine the items, you need to use these index values with the **get** function.

The following example shows the use of the **curselection** and **get** fuctions:

```perl
#!perl
#list2.pl

use Tk;

sub ok {
    $top = $main -> Toplevel();
    @elements = $lb -> curselection();
    $item = $lb -> get ($elements[0]);
    $lab1 = $top -> Label (
                -text => "$item",
                -background => $item) -> pack;
}

open (COLORS, "<rgb.txt") || die;
$temp=<COLORS>;  #need to remove 1st line
```

```perl
$main = MainWindow -> new;
$lb = $main -> Listbox -> pack;
while (<COLORS>) {
    chomp;
    s/^[0123456789 ]+//;
    s/\t\t//;
    $lb -> insert('end', $_);
}
$but = $main -> Button (-text => "Ok",
                        -command => sub {&ok}) -> pack;

MainLoop;
```

Output of list2.pl when program starts:

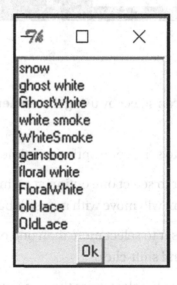

Output of list2.pl when a color is selected and the "Ok" button is pushed:

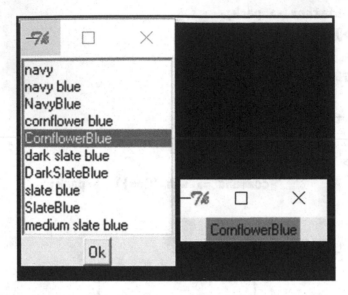

Selecting options

You can modify what the user can select by using the **-selectmode** option. The following options are permitted:

- **single** – Allows user to select one option at a time.

- **browse** – Allows user to select one option at a time. Differs from single in that selection will move with mouse if button 1 is held down.

- **extended** – Allows user to select more than one option at a time by using control-click and shift-click.

- **multiple** – Allows user to select more than one option at a time by clicking on additional items.

Selectmode example using the "multiple" option:

```perl
#!perl
#select1.pl
use Tk;
open (COLORS, "<rgb.txt") || die;
$temp=<COLORS>;   #need to remove 1st line
```

```perl
$main = MainWindow -> new;
$lb = $main -> Listbox (-selectmode => "multiple") -> pack;
while (<COLORS>) {
    chomp;
    s/^[0123456789 ]+//;
    s/\t\t//;
    $lb -> insert('end', $_);
}
MainLoop;
```

Output of select1.pl after three colors have been "clicked on":

The following program example of how the "extended" select mode works:

```perl
#!perl
#select2.pl

use Tk;

open (COLORS, "<rgb.txt") || die;

$temp=<COLORS>;   #need to remove 1st line

$main = MainWindow -> new;
$lb = $main -> Listbox (-selectmode => "extended") -> pack;
```

```
while (<COLORS>) {
    chomp;
    s/^[0123456789 ]+//;
    s/\t\t//;
    $lb -> insert('end', $_);
}

MainLoop;
```

Output of select2.pl after a "shift-click" method was used to select a block of colors:

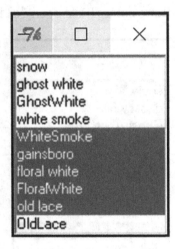

Scrollbars

When listboxes are too small to display all of the strings, scrollbars can be placed next to the listbox to provide the user a means of accessing the other strings. To create a scrollbar, use the following syntax:

```
$scroll = $main -> Scrollbar ('Widget', -scrollbars => 'value' [, options]);
```

Scrollbar example:

```perl
#!perl
#scroll.pl

use Tk;

open (COLORS, "<rgb.txt") || die;

$temp=<COLORS>;  #need to remove 1st line

$main = MainWindow -> new;
$scroll = $main->Scrollbar();
$lb = $main -> Listbox (
        -yscrollcommand => ['set' => $scroll]) -> pack(-side =>'left');
while (<COLORS>) {
   chomp;
   s/^[0123456789 ]+//;
   s/\t\t//;
   $lb -> insert('end', $_);
}

$scroll -> configure (-command => ['yview' => $lb]);

$scroll ->pack(-side => 'right', -fill => 'y');

MainLoop;
```

Notes about the program:

- The **-yscrollcommand** option to the listbox widget "links" the listbox with the $scroll scrollbar. The scrollbar will "listen" to directions from the listbox and move in sync with the listbox.

- The **-command** option that was used when configuring the scrollbar told the scrollbar to inform the $lb listbox of when to move its data.

- The **-side => 'left'** option told **pack** to place the listbox on the left-hand side of the window.

- The **-side => 'right'** option told **pack** to place the scrollbar on the right-hand side of the window.

- The **-fill => 'y'** option told pack to "fill out" the scrollbar vertically to match the side of the window.

Output of scroll.pl:

 **Try it!**

Perform the following steps:

- Open the widget program from the demos directory (this was covered in Chapter 10).

- Review the programs and the source code of the following:

  - The 50 states

  - Change widget's color scheme

  - A collection of famous and infamous sayings

```
Tk Perl/Tk Widget Demonstration          —    □    ×

File   Help
```

Listboxes

1. The 50 states.
2. Change widget's color scheme.
3. A collection of famous and infamous sayings.

Entries and Spin-boxes

1. Entries without scrollbars.
2. Entries with scrollbars.
3. Validated entries and password fields.
4. Spin-boxes.
5. Simple Rolodex-like form.

Text

1. Basic editable text.
2. Text display styles.
3. Hypertext (tag bindings).
4. A text widget with embedded windows.
5. A search tool built with a text widget.

Canvases

1. The canvas item types.
2. A simple 2-D plot.
3. Text items in canvases.
4. An editor for arrowheads on canvas lines.
5. A ruler with adjustable tab stops.
6. A building floor plan.
7. A simple scrollable canvas.
8. Tiles and transparent images.

Lab

Important note If you did not finish the previous lab, either finish it before starting this lab or use the completed `parse9-1.pl` provided in the lab answers folder.

Using code from `parse7.pl` and `parse9-1.pl`, generate a script that will perform the following operations:

- After the user answers the question provided by the toplevel, display the contents of the @proc array in the main window. Some thoughts regarding this:

  - Assume no data changes (ppid field gone, date change, etc.) have taken place yet.

  - Probably the best way to display the data in this case is as a listbox.

  - While you can use some of the code that you have in `parse7.pl`, the format statements you created won't be helpful. Now is a good time to explore the advantages of sprintf.

  - Don't worry about providing any "`header`" information at this time.

Store these changes in a file called `parse9-2.pl`.

When you have completed your work, compare your script against the `parse9-2.pl` file provided in lab answers.

Scales

Scale widgets are used to provide a sliding scale that the user can manipulate to choose a value. Use the following syntax to create a scale widget:

```perl
$scale = $parent -> Scale ( [option => value]) -> pack
```

Scale example:

```perl
#!perl
#scale1.pl

use Tk;

sub scale_remove {
    $tone = $scale -> get();
    $top -> destroy;
    $but2 -> configure (-text => "$tone");
```

```
}

sub tone {
    $top = $main -> Toplevel();
    $scale = $top -> Scale (-from => 0, -to => 100,
                                         -label => "Tone",
                                         -tickinterval => 10,
                                         -orient => "horizontal",
                                         -length => "6i") -> pack;
    $but1 = $top -> Button (-text => "Exit",
                                         -command => sub {scale_remove})
                                         -> pack;
}

$tone=0;
$main = MainWindow -> new;
$but1 = $main -> Button (-text => "Show scale",
                                         -command => sub {&tone}) -> pack;
$but2 = $main -> Button (-text => "$tone") -> pack;
$but3 = $main -> Button (-text => "Exit",
                                         -command => sub {exit}) -> pack;

MainLoop;
```

Notes about the program:

- The **-from** and **-to** options specify the "low" and "high" values.

- The **-tickinterval** option specifies where to set the tick marks.

- The statement **$tone = $scale -> get();** grabs the value that the scale is currently set to and assigns it to the variable $tone.

Output of **scale.pl**:

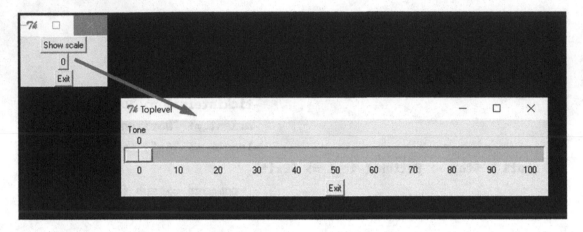

Setting a default scale value

To set a default value for a scale, use the **set** function. The following code demonstrates the use of this function:

```perl
#!perl
#scale2.pl

use Tk;

sub scale_remove {
    $tone = $scale -> get();
    $top -> destroy;
    $but2 -> configure (-text => "$tone");
}

sub tone {
    $top = $main -> Toplevel();
    $scale = $top -> Scale (-from => 0, -to => 100,
                                        -label => "Tone",
                                        -tickinterval => 10,
                                        -orient => "horizontal",
                                        -length => "6i") -> pack;
```

```perl
    $scale -> set(50);
    $but1 = $top -> Button (-text => "Exit",
                                        -command => sub {scale_remove})
                                        -> pack;
}

$tone=0;
$main = MainWindow -> new;
$but1 = $main -> Button (-text => "Show scale",
                                        -command => sub {&tone}) -> pack;
$but2 = $main -> Button (-text => "$tone") -> pack;
$but3 = $main -> Button (-text => "Exit",
                                        -command => sub {exit}) -> pack;

MainLoop;
```

Try it!

Perform the following steps:

- Open the widget program from the demos directory (this was covered in Chapter 10).

- Review the programs and the source code of the following:

    - Horizontal scale

    - Vertical scale

76 Perl/Tk Widget Demonstration   —   ☐   ✕

File   Help

Scales

    1. Horizontal scale.
    2. Vertical scale.

Paned Windows

    1. Horizontal paned window.
    2. Vertical paned window.

Photos and Images

    1. Transparent pixels.
    2. Alpha channel compositing.

Menus

    1. Menus and cascades (sub-menus).
    2. As above, but using Perl/Tk -menuitems.
    3. Menubuttons.

Common Dialogs

    1. Message boxes.
    2. File selection dialog.
    3. Directory selection dialog.
    4. Color picker.

Tix Widgets

    1. Popup help window when mouse lingers over widget.
    2. Entry with Listbox to select list values.

Entries

Entries are used to allow the user to type in data that will be assigned to a variable. Use the following syntax to create a scale widget:

```
$entry = $parent -> Entry ( [option => value]) -> pack
```

An entry example:

```perl
#!perl
#entry1.pl

use Tk;

sub entry_remove {
    $tone = $entry -> get();
    $top -> destroy;
    $but2 -> configure (-text => "$tone");
}

sub tone {
    $top = $main -> Toplevel();
    $lab1 = $top -> Label (-text => "Enter Tone:") -> pack;
    $entry = $top -> Entry -> pack;
    $but1 = $top -> Button (-text => "Exit",
                                       -command => sub {entry_remove})
                                       -> pack;
}

$tone=0;
$main = MainWindow -> new;
$but1 = $main -> Button (-text => "Enter tone",
                                       -command => sub {&tone}) -> pack;
$but2 = $main -> Button (-text => "$tone") -> pack;
$but3 = $main -> Button (-text => "Exit",
                                       -command => sub {exit}) -> pack;

MainLoop;
```

Output of entry1.pl:

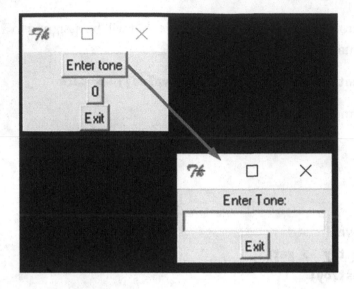

Hiding the user's input

Suppose you are having the user type in a password. For security reasons, you don't want to have the user's password display as they are typing. To hide the user's input, use the -**show** option:

```perl
#!perl
#entry2.pl

use Tk;

sub entry_remove {
    $tone = $entry -> get();          $top -> destroy;
    $but2 -> configure (-text => "$tone");
}

sub tone {
    $top = $main -> Toplevel();
    $lab1 = $top -> Label (-text => "Enter Tone:") -> pack;
    $entry = $top -> Entry (-show => "*") -> pack;
```

```perl
    $but1 = $top -> Button (-text => "Exit",
                                          -command => sub {entry_remove})
                                          -> pack;
}

$tone=0;   $main = MainWindow -> new;
$but1 = $main -> Button (-text => "Enter tone",
                                          -command => sub {&tone}) -> pack;
$but2 = $main -> Button (-text => "$tone") -> pack;
$but3 = $main -> Button (-text => "Exit",
                                          -command => sub {exit}) -> pack;

MainLoop;
```

Output of entry2.pl (note the * characters in the "Enter Tone:" entry box):

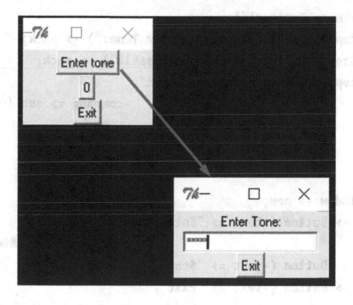

Disable an entry box

In some cases, you may want to display an entry box but not allow the user to enter data. To do this, use the **-state** option:

```perl
#!perl
#entry3.pl

use Tk;

sub entry_remove {
    $tone = $entry -> get();      $top -> destroy;
    $but2 -> configure (-text => "$tone");
}

sub tone {
    $top = $main -> Toplevel();
    $lab1 = $top -> Label (-text => "Enter Tone:") -> pack;
    $entry = $top -> Entry (-state => "disable") -> pack;
    $but1 = $top -> Button (-text => "Exit",
                                        -command => sub {entry_remove})
                                        -> pack;

}

$tone=0;
$main = MainWindow -> new;
$but1 = $main -> Button (-text => "Enter tone",
                                    -command => sub {&tone}) -> pack;
$but2 = $main -> Button (-text => "$tone") -> pack;
$but3 = $main -> Button (-text => "Exit",
                                    -command => sub {exit}) -> pack;

MainLoop;
```

Output of `entry3.pl` (note that the "Enter Tone:" entry box is "grayed out"):

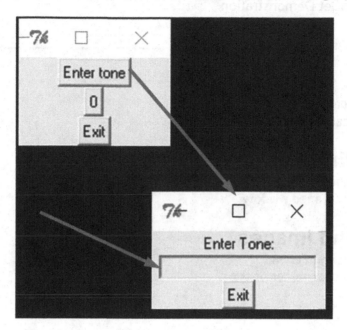

 **Try it!**

Perform the following steps:

- Open the widget program from the demos directory (this was covered in Chapter 10).

- Review the programs and the source code of the following:

    - Message boxes

    - File selection dialog

    - Directory selection dialog

    - Color picker

Tk Perl/Tk Widget Demonstration   — ☐ ✕

File   Help

Scales

    1. Horizontal scale.
    2. Vertical scale.

Paned Windows

    1. Horizontal paned window.
    2. Vertical paned window.

Photos and Images

    1. Transparent pixels.
    2. Alpha channel compositing.

Menus

    1. Menus and cascades (sub-menus).
    2. As above, but using Perl/Tk -menuitems.
    3. Menubuttons.

Common Dialogs

    1. Message boxes.
    2. File selection dialog.
    3. Directory selection dialog.
    4. Color picker.

Tix Widgets

    1. Popup help window when mouse lingers over widget.
    2. Entry with Listbox to select list values.

Creating menus

Menus are the most complex of the widgets. This chapter covers the different options (or entries) available in creating menus including

- Check entries to select multiple options (like checkbuttons)
- Radio entries to select one option (like radiobuttons)
- Separators to separate different options
- Command entries to invoke a procedure or other perl code
- Cascade entries to display submenus

Creating the menu options

To create a menu, first create a frame to place the menu in. You will most likely also want to create another larger frame to put the rest of the application.

The following syntax is used to create a menu:

```
$menu = $frame -> Menubutton (-text => "text") -> pack
```

The following program will create a basic menu. **Note**: Since no action has been assigned to the menu options (yet), TK will produce an error if you try to click a menu option:

```
#!perl
#menu1.pl

use Tk;

$main = MainWindow -> new;

$frame1 = $main -> Frame (-relief => groove,
                          -borderwidth => 3) -> pack (-fill => "x");
$frame2 = $main -> Frame (-height => 150, -width => 200) -> pack;

$File_menu = $frame1 -> Menubutton (-text => "File")
                                    -> pack (-side => "left");
$Edit_menu = $frame1 -> Menubutton (-text => "Edit")
                                    -> pack (-side => "left");
```

```perl
$Help_menu = $frame1 -> Menubutton (-text => "Help")
                                        -> pack (-side => "right");

MainLoop;
```

Output for menu1.pl:

Adding radio options

Now that we have the basic menu, we can add options to the menu. You can have these options execute a command or display a check or radio submenu.

The following example will add radio buttons to the Edit menu:

```perl
#!perl
#menu2.pl

use Tk;

sub set_color {$frame2 -> configure (-background => $background); }

$main = MainWindow -> new;

$frame1 = $main -> Frame (-relief => groove,
                                        -borderwidth => 3)
                        -> pack (-fill => "x");
$frame2 = $main -> Frame (-height => 150, -width => 200) -> pack;

$File_menu = $frame1 -> Menubutton (-text => "File")
                                    -> pack (-side => "left");
```

```perl
$Edit_menu = $frame1 -> Menubutton (-text => "Edit")
                                    -> pack (-side => "left");
$Help_menu = $frame1 -> Menubutton (-text => "Help")
                                    -> pack (-side => "right");

foreach $color (red, green, blue, yellow, black, white) {
    $Edit_menu -> radiobutton (-label => $color,
                                    -command => \&set_color,
                                    -variable => \$background,
                                    -value => $color)
}

MainLoop;
```

Output of menu2.pl when program starts:

Output of menu2.pl when "Edit" menu button is clicked:

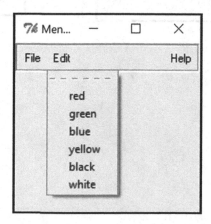

283

Output of menu2.pl when "red" option button is clicked:

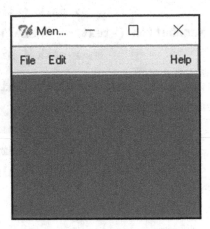

Note that the submenu has a feature called a "tearoff". By clicking the "-----"
above the options, a toplevel window is automatically created:

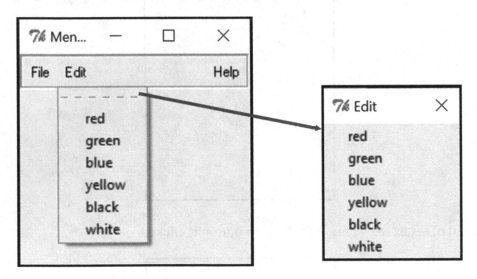

Adding check options

In the next example, checkbutton options are added to the Edit menu:

```perl
#!perl
#menu3.pl

use Tk;
sub info {$lab1 = $main -> Label (-bitmap => 'info') -> pack;}
sub error {$lab1 = $main -> Label (-bitmap => 'error') -> pack;}
sub warn {$lab1 = $main -> Label (-bitmap => 'warning') -> pack;}
$main = MainWindow -> new;

$frame1 = $main -> Frame (-relief => groove, -borderwidth => 3)
                                    -> pack (-fill => "x");
$frame2 = $main -> Frame (-height => 150, -width => 200) -> pack;
$File_menu = $frame1 -> Menubutton (-text => "File")
                                        -> pack (-side => "left");
$Edit_menu = $frame1 -> Menubutton (-text => "Edit")
                                        -> pack (-side => "left");
$Help_menu = $frame1 -> Menubutton (-text => "Help")
                                        -> pack (-side => "right");

$Edit_menu -> checkbutton (-label => "Show info",
                                    -variable => \$info,
                                    -command => sub {if
                                    ($info) {&info}});

$Edit_menu -> checkbutton (-label => "Show error",
                                    -variable => \$error,
                                    -command => sub {if
                                    ($error) {&error}});

$Edit_menu -> checkbutton (-label => "Show warning",
                                    -variable => \$warn,
                                    -command => sub {
                                        if ($warn) {&warn}});

MainLoop;
```

285

Output of menu3.pl when program starts:

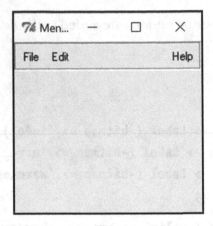

Output of menu3.pl when the "Edit" menubutton is clicked:

Output of menu3.pl when the "Show info" is clicked:

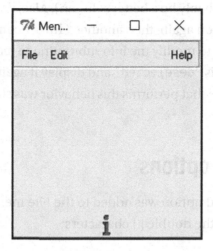

Notes about menu3.pl:

- The "info" icon appears at the bottom because it was packed under the frame defined in the $frame2 variable. It might be better in this case to put it within the frame defined by the $frame2 variable.

- Note that once the "Show info" option is chosen, there is a check box next to this option:

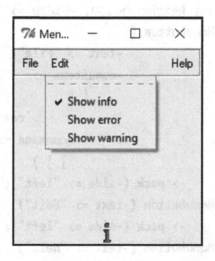

- If you "deselect" the "Show info" option, the info icon isn't removed (which would probably be a better solution). Also, if you "select" the "Show info" option again, then another "info" icon will appear. It would be better to modify the info subroutine to remove the "info" icon if the option is "deselected" and display it again if the option is "selected". Code that performs this behavior was shown earlier in this chapter.

Adding command options

In this example, a command option was added to the File menu. Note that "menuitems" is an array of arrays, hence the double [ ] characters:

```perl
#!perl
#menu4.pl

use Tk;

$main = MainWindow -> new;

$frame1 = $main -> Frame (-relief => groove, -borderwidth => 3) -> pack
(-fill => "x");
$frame2 = $main -> Frame (-height => 150, -width => 200) -> pack;
$File_menu = $frame1 -> Menubutton (
                              -text => "File",
                              -menuitems =>
                                 [ [
                                            'command' => "Exit",
                                      -command => sub {$main -> destroy}
                                    ] ] )
                       -> pack (-side => "left");
$Edit_menu = $frame1 -> Menubutton (-text => "Edit")
                       -> pack (-side => "left");
$Help_menu = $frame1 -> Menubutton (-text => "Help")
                       -> pack (-side => "right");

MainLoop;
```

Output of `menu4.pl` when the "File" menubutton is pressed:

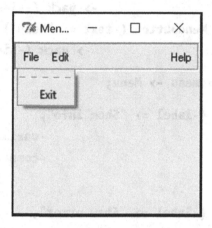

Adding cascade and separators

In addition to radio, check, and command options, you can add a cascade option and separators. A cascade option will open a submenu that will contain additional options. A separator will break up options.

The following example illustrates how cascade options and separators are used:

```perl
#!perl
#menu5.pl

use Tk;
sub set_color {$frame2 -> configure (-background => $background);}
sub info {$lab1 = $main -> Label (-bitmap => 'info') -> pack;}
sub error {$lab1 = $main -> Label (-bitmap => 'error') -> pack;}
sub warn {$lab1 = $main -> Label (-bitmap => 'warning') -> pack;}
$main = MainWindow -> new;

$frame1 = $main -> Frame (-relief => groove, -borderwidth => 3)
                                -> pack (-fill => "x");
$frame2 = $main -> Frame (-height => 150, -width => 200) -> pack;
$File_menu = $frame1 -> Menubutton (-text => "File")
                                        -> pack (-side => "left");
```

```perl
$Edit_menu = $frame1 -> Menubutton (-text => "Edit")
                                        -> pack (-side => "left");
$Help_menu = $frame1 -> Menubutton (-text => "Help")
                                        -> pack (-side => "right");

$subshow = $Edit_menu -> menu -> Menu;

$subshow -> checkbutton (-label => "Show info",
                                        -variable => \$info,
                                        -command => sub {
                                            if ($info) {&info}});

$subshow -> checkbutton (-label => "Show error",
                                        -variable => \$error,
                                        -command => sub {
                                            if ($error) {&error}});

$subshow -> checkbutton (-label => "Show warning",
                                        -variable => \$warn,
                                        -command => sub {
                                            if ($warn) {&warn}});

$subcolor = $Edit_menu -> menu -> Menu;

foreach $color (red, green, blue, yellow, black, white) {
    $subcolor -> radiobutton (-label => $color,
                                        -command => \&set_color,
                                        -variable => \$background,
                                        -value => $color)
}

$Edit_menu -> cascade (-label => "Show");
$Edit_menu -> entryconfigure("Show", -menu => $subshow);

$Edit_menu -> separator();

$Edit_menu -> cascade (-label => "Color");
$Edit_menu -> entryconfigure("Color", -menu => $subcolor);

MainLoop;
```

Notes about `menu5.pl`:

- The line "`$subshow = $Edit_menu -> menu -> Menu;`" defines a submenu.

- The line "`$Edit_menu -> cascade (-label => "Show");`" tells TK that there is a cascade menu that will be associated with the $Edit_menu option.

- The line "`$Edit_menu -> entryconfigure("Show", -menu => $subshow);`" associates the submenu with the cascade.

Output of `menu5.pl`:

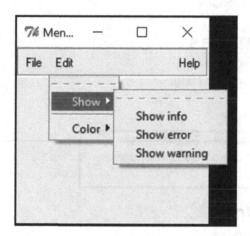

Try it!

Perform the following steps:

- Open the widget program from the demos directory (this was covered in Chapter 10).

- Review the programs and the source code of the following:

  - Menus and cascades (submenus)

  - As above but with Perl/Tk -menuitems

  - Menubuttons

Perl/Tk Widget Demonstration   —   □   ✕

File   Help

Scales
1. Horizontal scale.
2. Vertical scale.

Paned Windows
1. Horizontal paned window.
2. Vertical paned window.

Photos and Images
1. Transparent pixels.
2. Alpha channel compositing.

Menus
1. Menus and cascades (sub-menus).
2. As above, but using Perl/Tk -menuitems.
3. Menubuttons.

Common Dialogs
1. Message boxes.
2. File selection dialog.
3. Directory selection dialog.
4. Color picker.

Tix Widgets
1. Popup help window when mouse lingers over widget.
2. Entry with Listbox to select list values.

Additional resources

In each chapter, resources are provided to provide the learner with a source for more information. These resources may include downloadable source code or links to other books or articles that will provide you more information about the topic at hand.

Resources for this chapter can be found here:

```
https://github.com/Apress/pro-perl-programming
```

Lab exercises

Important note If you did not finish the previous lab, either finish it before starting this lab or use the completed `parse9-2.pl` provided in the lab answers folder.

Using code from `parse9-2.pl`, generate a script that will perform the following operations:

- Have a menu bar within a frame. Have the menu bar have two items: File and Filter.

- Create a menu item for File that will exit the program.

- Create a menu item for Filter for each of the filter features:

  - Remove newline characters.

  - Convert date.

  - Remove PPID field.

- Place the listbox that displays the data in a frame under the menu bar. If the user chooses a filter option, update the data as needed.

Store these changes in a file called `parse9-3.pl`.

When you have completed your work, compare your script against the `parse9-3.pl` file provided in lab answers.

CHAPTER 12

Geometry Managers

During the last two chapters, the focus has been on creating widgets. Now we will focus on how to place (manipulate) widgets in the window. The **pack** command is used to determine where widgets go and how big they will be.

It is important to understand that **pack** controls the size and location of the widgets; the widgets themselves do not have the ultimate control of these parameters. For example, if a widget definition "requests" to be 2 inches wide and 3 inches tall, **pack** will accommodate this request unless an option is passed to **pack** to override the request. When a conflict like this occurs, the **pack** specifications "wins".

The -after and -before option

By default, widgets are placed in the order that they are packed. You can override this by using the **-after** or **-before** options. The syntax of these options is

```
$widget -> pack (-after | -before => $otherwidget)
```

In the following example, the -after option is used to place the frame defined by the $frame5 variable after the frame defined by the $frame2 variable. To make it easier to see the result, the size and color of the defined by the $frame5 variable are different than all of the other frames:

```
#!perl
#after.pl
```

© William "Bo" Rothwell of One Course Source, Inc. 2020
W. "Bo" Rothwell, *Pro Perl Programming*, https://doi.org/10.1007/978-1-4842-5605-3_12

```perl
use Tk;

$main = MainWindow -> new;
$frame1 = $main -> Frame (-relief => raised, -height => 100,
                                            -width => 200, -borderwidth
                                            => 15) ->pack;
$frame2 = $main -> Frame (-relief => sunken, -height => 100,
                                            -width => 200, -borderwidth
                                            => 15) ->pack;
$frame3 = $main -> Frame (-relief => flat, -height => 100,
                                            -width => 200, -borderwidth
                                            => 15) ->pack;
$frame4 = $main -> Frame (-relief => groove, -height => 100,
                                            -width => 200, -borderwidth
                                            => 15) ->pack;
$frame5 = $main -> Frame (-relief => ridge, -height => 250,
                                            -width => 200, -borderwidth
                                            => 15,
                                            -background => "blue")
                        ->pack (-after => $frame2);

MainLoop;
```

Output of `after.pl`:

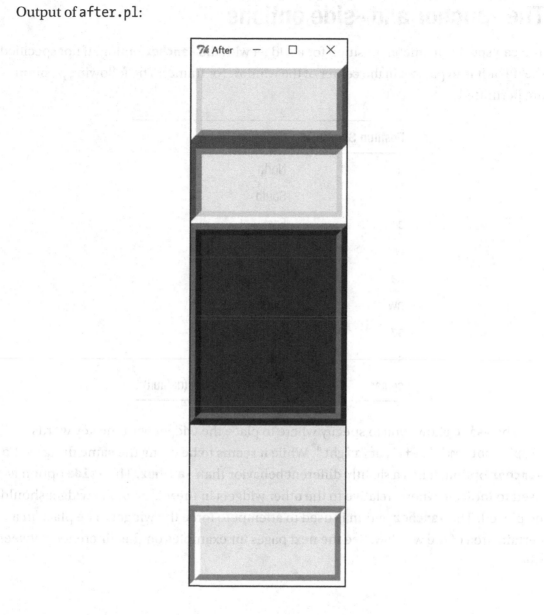

The -anchor and -side options

You can specify an anchor position for a widget with the **-anchor** option. If not specified, the default is to place it in the center of the window (or frame). The following positions are permitted:

Position Symbol	Location
n	North
s	South
e	East
w	West
ne	Northeast
nw	Northwest
se	Southeast
sw	Southwest
center	Center of window (default)

The **-side** allows you to specify where to place the widget with the key words "top", "bottom", "left", or "right". While it seems to be doing the same thing as the **-anchor** option, it has a slightly different behavior than **-anchor**. The **-side** option is used to indicate where, relative to the other widgets in the window, the widget should be placed. The **-anchor** option is used to attempt to force the widget to be place in a certain area of the window. See the next pages for examples on the difference between the two.

-anchor vs. -side

In the following example, widgets will be placed, in order, from top to bottom. Two of the widgets will be anchored on the west side of the window, and one will be anchored on the east side of the window.

```perl
#!perl
#side1.pl

use Tk;

$main = MainWindow -> new;

$but1 = $main -> Button (-text => "Show info")
                        -> pack (-side => top, -anchor => w);
$but2 = $main -> Button (-text => "Show error")
                        -> pack(-side => top, -anchor => e);
$but3 = $main -> Button (-text => "Show warning")
                        -> pack(-side => top, -anchor => w);

MainLoop;
```

Output of side1.pl when program starts:

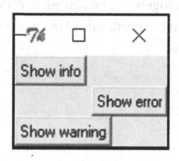

Notice how the anchoring affects the position of the widgets when the overall window is resized:

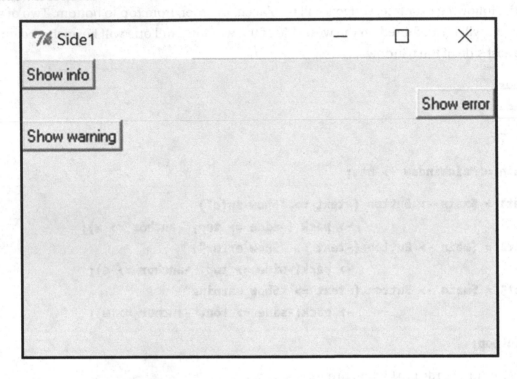

In the following example, widgets will be placed, in order, from right to left. Two of the widgets will be anchored on the north side of the window, and one will be anchored on the south side of the window.

```perl
#!perl
#side2.pl

use Tk;

$main = MainWindow -> new;

$but1 = $main -> Button (-text => "Show info")
                    -> pack (-side => "right", -anchor => "n");
$but2 = $main -> Button (-text => "Show error")
                    -> pack(-side => "right", -anchor => "s");
$but3 = $main -> Button (-text => "Show warning")
                    -> pack(-side => "right", -anchor => "n");

MainLoop;
```

Output of `side2.pl` when program is started:

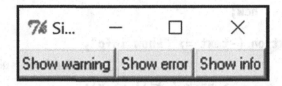

Notice how the anchoring affects the position of the widgets when the overall window is resized:

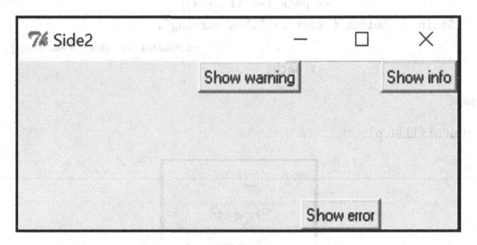

The `-fill` option

If the widget is too small to fill the frame it is in, you can specify the **-fill** option to have the widget grow to fit the frame.

With **-fill** you can indicate that you want the widget to fill in horizontally, vertically, or both. The syntax for this option is

The option can be either an "x" (horizontal fill), a "y" (vertical fill), or "both" (fill horizontally and vertically).

Fill example:

```perl
#!perl
#fill1.pl

use Tk;

sub info {$lab1 = $main -> Label (-bitmap => 'info') -> pack;}
sub error {$lab2 = $main -> Label (-bitmap => 'error') -> pack;}
```

301

```perl
sub warning {$lab3 = $main -> Label (-bitmap => 'warning') -> pack;}

$main = MainWindow -> new;

$but1 = $main -> Button (-text => "Show info",
                                        -command => sub {&info})
                        -> pack (-fill => x);
$but2 = $main -> Button (-text => "Show error",
                                        -command => sub {&error})
                        -> pack (-fill => x);
$but3 = $main -> Button (-text => "Show warning",
                                        -command => sub {&warning})
                        -> pack;

MainLoop;
```

Output of fill1.pl:

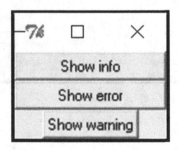

Note that the "Show warning" button didn't have the -fill option, so it was only as big as necessary to fit the text that is in the button. Also note that when the window is resized, the buttons that have the -fill option defined also increase in size:

Also note that the buttons don't change size when the window is resized vertically:

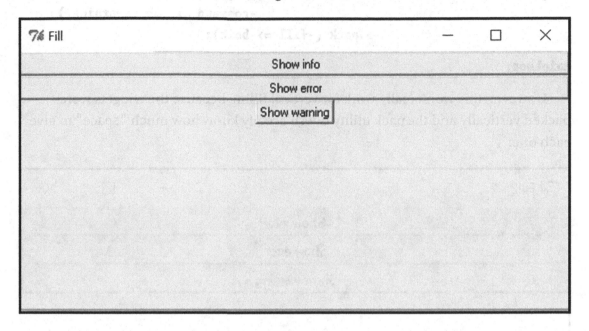

You could fill both vertically and horizontally:

```perl
#!perl
#fill2.pl

use Tk;

sub info {$lab1 = $main -> Label (-bitmap => 'info') -> pack;}
sub error {$lab2 = $main -> Label (-bitmap => 'error') -> pack;}
sub warning {$lab3 = $main -> Label (-bitmap => 'warning') -> pack;}

$main = MainWindow -> new;

$but1 = $main -> Button (-text => "Show info",
                                      -command => sub {&info})
                -> pack (-fill => both);
$but2 = $main -> Button (-text => "Show error",
                                      -command => sub {&error})
                -> pack (-fill => both);
```

```
$but3 = $main -> Button (-text => "Show warning",
                                  -command => sub {&warning})
                -> pack (-fill => both);

MainLoop;
```

However, this won't really work for vertical filling because the widgets were packed vertically and the pack utility doesn't really know how much "space" to give each one:

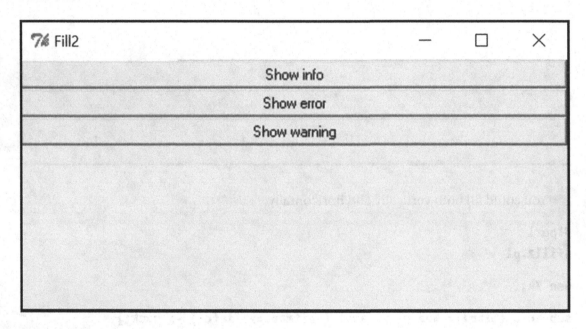

Filling both vertically and horizontally normally only works well when there is a single widget in the window or frame.

Padding with pack

You can specify either internal or external padding for widgets with the pack command. The following chart illustrates the different padding options:

Padding Option	Meaning
-ipadx *amount*	Pad widget horizontal borders internally by *amount*
-ipady *amount*	Pad widget vertical borders internally by *amount*
-padx *amount*	Pad widget horizontal borders external by *amount*
-pady *amount*	Pad widget vertical borders externally by *amount*

The *amount* can be specified by any of the following units:

- Centimeters – "c"

- Inches – "i"

- Millimeters – "m"

- Points – "p"

Padding example:

```perl
#!perl
#ppad.pl

use Tk;

sub info {$lab1 = $main -> Label (-bitmap => 'info') -> pack;}
sub error {$lab2 = $main -> Label (-bitmap => 'error') -> pack;}
sub warning {$lab3 = $main -> Label (-bitmap => 'warning') -> pack;}

$main = MainWindow -> new;

$but1 = $main -> Button (-text => "Show info",
                                        -command => sub {&info})
                    -> pack (-ipadx => 10, -ipady => 10);
$but2 = $main -> Button (-text => "Show error",
                                          -command => sub {&error})
                    -> pack (-padx => 10, -pady => 10);
$but3 = $main -> Button (-text => "Show warning",
                                          -command => sub {&warning})
                    -> pack;

MainLoop;
```

Output of `ppad.pl`:

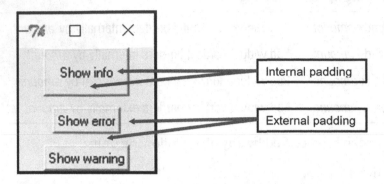

Managing widgets with pack

If you start combining different side and/or position options when packing widgets, you will find that the result can be quite weird. For example, look at the following program and the output it produces:

```perl
#!perl
#weird.pl

use Tk;

$main = MainWindow -> new;

$frame1 = $main -> Frame (-relief => raised, -height => 150,
                                            -width => 200,
                                            -borderwidth => 15,
                                            -background => blue)
                    ->pack (-side => "left");
$frame2 = $main -> Frame (-relief => sunken, -height => 150,
                                            -width => 200,
                                            -borderwidth => 15,
                                            -background => black)
                    ->pack (-anchor => "e");
```

```
$frame3 = $main -> Frame (-relief => flat, -height => 150,
                                         -width => 200,
                                         -borderwidth => 15,
                                         -background => yellow)
                    ->pack (-side => "top");
$frame4 = $main -> Frame (-relief => groove, -height => 150,
                                         -width => 200,
                                         -borderwidth => 15,
                                         -background => green)
                    ->pack (-side => "bottom", -fill => "both");
$frame5 = $main -> Frame (-relief => ridge, -height => 150,
                                         -width => 200,
                                         -borderwidth => 15,
                                         -background => purple)
                    ->pack (-side => "left");

MainLoop;
```

Output of `weird.pl`:

This is probably NOT what you wanted TK to do. Granted, it isn't too crazy…yet. Try running the program and then resizing the window:

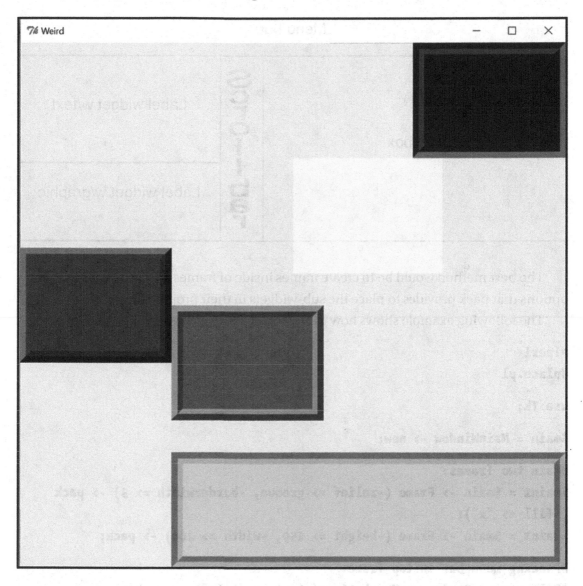

The process of organizing widgets involves good use of frames. For example, suppose we want to make the following window:

Menu bar		
List box	S c r o l l b a r	Label widget w/text
		Label widget w/graphic

The best method would be to create frames inside of frames and use the placement options that pack provides to place the sub-widgets in their proper place.

The following example shows how to create this more complex widget structure:

```perl
#!perl
#place.pl

use Tk;

$main = MainWindow -> new;

#Main two frames:
$main1 = $main -> Frame (-relief => groove, -borderwidth => 3) -> pack
(-fill => "x");
$main2 = $main -> Frame (-height => 150, -width => 200) -> pack;

#Placing menu bar in top frame:
$File_menu = $main1 -> Menubutton (-text => "File") -> pack
(-side => "left");
$Edit_menu = $main1 -> Menubutton (-text => "Edit") -> pack
(-side => "left");
$Help_menu = $main1 -> Menubutton (-text => "Help") -> pack
(-side => "right");
```

```perl
#Breaking up bottom frame:
$sub1 = $main2 -> Frame -> pack (-side => "left");
$sub2 = $main2 -> Frame -> pack (-side => "right");

#Putting Listbox in left frame:
open (COLORS, "<rgb.txt") || die;
$temp=<COLORS>;   #need to remove 1st line

$scroll = $sub1->Scrollbar();
$lb = $sub1 -> Listbox (-yscrollcommand => ['set' => $scroll])
            -> pack(-side=> 'left');

while (<COLORS>) {
    chomp;
    s/^[0123456789 ]+//;
    s/\t\t//;
    $lb -> insert('end', $_);
}

$scroll -> configure (-command => ['yview' => $lb]);
$scroll ->pack(-side => 'right', -fill => 'y');

#Placing labels in right frame:
$lab1 = $sub2 -> Label (
            -text => "Perl is the best",
            -font =>
            '-adobe-courier-medium-o-normal--24-240-75-75-m-150-hp-roman8')
            -> pack;
$lab2 = $sub2 -> Label (-bitmap => 'questhead') -> pack;

MainLoop;
```

Output of `place.pl`

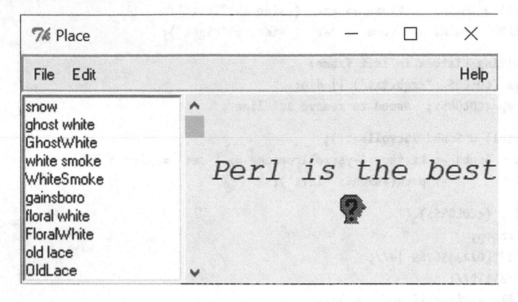

Binding

Binding is the process of associating widgets with *events*. An *event* can be a keyboard key being pressed, mouse clicking, mouse movement (leaving and entering widgets), widget size changing, widgets being destroyed, and other actions.

The topic of binding is a huge one; only the basics of binding will be discussed in this unit

The format of bind is

```
$widget -> bind (event, action)
```

event

An event is a series of mouse or keyboard actions. An event is broken down into two categories: modifier and event type.

The following chart illustrates the possible modifiers:

Modifiers	Meaning
Control	The control key
Shift	The shift key

(continued)

Modifiers	Meaning
Lock	The Caps Lock key
Alt	The Alt key
Double	Double-pressed events (normally for double-clicking)
Triple	Triple-pressed events (normally for triple-clicking)
Button #	Which button (1, left; 2, center; 3,right)

The following chart illustrates the possible event types:

Event Type	Meaning
ButtonPress	A button is pressed
ButtonRelease	A button is released
Destroy	The window is destroyed
Enter	The mouse has entered the window
KeyPress	A key is pressed
KeyRelease	A key is released
Leave	A mouse is leaving the window

The two event types we will focus on will be "ButtonPress" and "KeyPress" as they are the most common.

To specify which button (left, center, or right), specify the number of the button:

<ButtonPress-1>	Left button
<ButtonPress-2>	Center button
<ButtonPress-3>	Right button

To specify which key, specify the key after the "KeyPress" event type:

<KeyPress-a>	The "a" key
<KeyPress-z>	The "z" key
<KeyPress-Return>	The "return" key

313

Other special keys can be specified: Escape, Backspace, Tab, Up, Down, Left, Right, comma, period, dollar, number sign.

You can also specify event modifiers. For example, maybe you want an action to take place if the user holds down the control button and presses the "a" key.

Examples:

          <Control-KeyPress-a>   Control+a

          <Double-ButtonPress-1>   Double-click the left mouse button

The following example will bind the left mouse button to the **destroy** command. The **destroy** command will delete widgets.

```perl
#!perl
#bind.pl

use Tk;

$main = MainWindow -> new;
$main -> bind ("<ButtonPress-1>", sub {destroy $main});

$lab1 = $main -> Label (-text => "Perl is the best",
                                        -font => '-adobe-courier-medium-o-
normal--24-240-75-75-m-150-hp-roman8')
            -> pack;

$lab2 = $main -> Label (-text => "Don't you think?",
                                        -font => '-adobe-helvetica-medium-
                                        o-normal--24-240-75-75-p-130-
                                        iso8859-1')
            -> pack;

MainLoop;
```

Output of bind.pl (run this and then click anywhere in the main window to see the program exit):

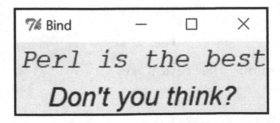

The focus command

If you want the user to be able to use the keyboard keys to enact commands in other widgets, you have to use the **focus** command. The **focus** command tells TK what window to "focus on" when looking for keyboard input.

The following example will switch the focus of the keyboard to the entry widget:

```perl
#!perl
#focus.pl

use Tk;

sub entry_remove {
    $tone = $entry -> get();
    $top -> destroy;
    $but2 -> configure (-text => "$tone");
}

sub tone {
    $top = $main -> Toplevel();
    $lab1 = $top -> Label (-text => "Enter Tone:") -> pack;
    $entry = $top -> Entry -> pack;
    $entry -> focus();
    $but1 = $top -> Button (-text => "Exit",
                                        -command => sub {entry_remove})
                -> pack;}

$tone=0;
$main = MainWindow -> new;

$but1 = $main -> Button (-text => "Enter tone",
                                        -command => sub {&tone})
            -> pack;
$but2 = $main -> Button (-text => "$tone") -> pack;
$but3 = $main -> Button (-text => "Exit", -command => sub {exit})
            -> pack;

MainLoop;
```

To see how the focus.pl program works, first run the program and then click the "Enter tone" button:

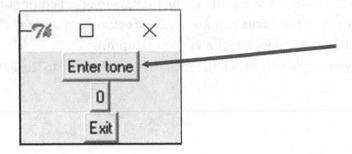

Note that you can start typing the tone value immediately, without having to click in window:

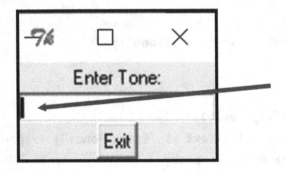

Try it!

Another popular geometry manager is call canvas. Perform the following steps for a quick introduction to the canvas geometry manager:

- Open the widget program from the demos directory (this was covered in Chapter 10).
- Review the programs and the source code of the following:
  - The canvas item types
  - A simple 2-D plot
  - Test items in canvases
  - An editor for arrowheads on canvas lines

- A ruler with adjustable tab stops

- A building floor plan

- A simple scrollable canvas

- Tiles and transparent images

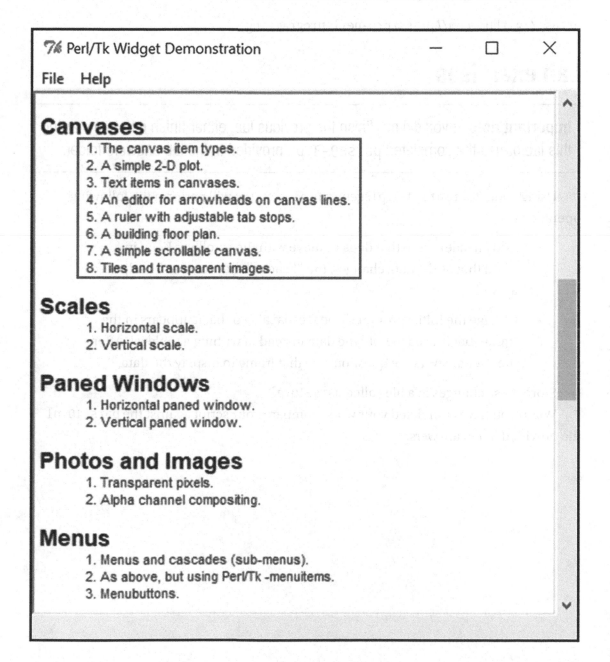

Additional resources

In each chapter, resources are provided to provide the learner with a source for more information. These resources may include downloadable source code or links to other books or articles that will provide you more information about the topic at hand.

Resources for this chapter can be found here:

```
https://github.com/Apress/pro-perl-programming
```

Lab exercises

Important note If you did not finish the previous lab, either finish it before starting this lab or use the completed `parse9-3.pl` provided in the lab answers folder.

Using code from `parse9-3.pl`, generate a script that will perform the following operations:

- Add "`header`" info that doesn't move with the scrollbar. Keep in mind that as the data changes, the "`header`" may need to be adjusted as well.

- Change the initial prompt ("`Update data`") so that it appears in the frame that is used to hold the data instead of withing a toplevel. After the user answers the question, use that frame to display the data.

Store these changes in a file called `parse10.pl`.

When you have completed your work, compare your script against the `parse10.pl` file provided in lab answers.

Index

Symbol

@ARGV array, 126
$ARGV variable, 125
$^E variable, 135, 136
=> operator, 89
<> operator, 125
? metacharacters, 7
| metacharacters, 12
^ and $ metacharacters, 11
* and + metacharacters, 5
? metacharacters, 7
. metacharacters, 8
( ) metacharacters, 11, 12
[ ] metacharacters, 8, 9
{ } metacharacters, 6, 7
^* placeholder, 120
$! variable, 135
$? variable, 133–135
$@ variable, 136

A

\A assertion, 33, 47
ActiveState debugger, 217
Array context, 74
Assertions, 27
    g modifier, 29
    look forward/back, 27, 29
autouse pragma, 182

B

B command, 213, 214
B * command, 215
Backreference patterns, 15–18
Backtracking, 66, 67
Benchmark module, 57, 58, 196, 197
Binding
    ButtonPress, 313
    event, 312, 313
    KeyPress, 313
    modifiers, 312, 313
-borderwidth
    option, 236
Built-in Perl modules
    drawbacks, 185
    @INC variable, 180, 181
    location of loaded, 181
    use autouse pragma, 182
Built-in variables
    English names, 132
    reference chart, 129–131
Buttons
    cursor,
        change, 251, 252
    destroy, 249–250
    exit application, 248, 249
    lab, 254, 255
    toplevels, 252, 253
    types, 247

© William "Bo" Rothwell of One Course Source, Inc. 2020
W. "Bo" Rothwell, *Pro Perl Programming*, https://doi.org/10.1007/978-1-4842-5605-3

Printed in the United States
By Bookmasters